THE COUNTRY PARSON

THE COUNTRY PARSON

GOD'S COUNTRY

The Gracewing Rural Life Anthologies
Series editor: Leslie J. Francis

THE COUNTRY PARSON
Leslie J. Francis

For
Ronald Arthur Francis
(3rd October 1911—1st October 1987)
who always supported my vocation to be
a country parson

.

Fowler Wright Books
Old URC Church
Burgess Street
Leominster HR6 8DE

First published 1989
ISBN 085 244 150 9

Compilation, introduction and commentary copyright © Leslie J. Francis, 1989
Illustrations copyright © Fowler Wright Books, 1989
Copyright information for individual extracts is given on appropriate pages
No part of this work may be reproduced without permission

Typeset by Print Origination (NW) Limited, Formby, L37 8EG
Printed in Great Britain by Billings & Sons Limited, Worcester

CONTENTS

FOREWORD

by His Grace the Archbishop of Wales

Ever since the days of George Herbert the country parson has been seen as the guardian of some of the essential qualities of Anglicanism. Those of us who have served a part of our ministry in rural areas are aware of the close relationship which a country pastor can build up with all sections of the community which he serves.

In this fascinating and wide-ranging anthology Leslie Francis draws on literary, biographical and autobiographical sources to present a portrait of the country clergyman with all his strengths and weaknesses. The picture is very much an English one (Welsh country clergy are a wholly different breed, as readers of Canon D. Parry-Jones's *Welsh Country Parson* will know) — but the book is no less enjoyable for that.

With recent changes in the deployment of clergy the country parson has often seemed in danger of becoming virtually extinct. Towards the end of this anthology Leslie Francis includes extracts from various different visions and models for future rural ministry, some of them radical in the extreme. Whatever the future may hold, however, one thing is certain: Anglicanism will always have a special place in the rural life of England and Wales and the insights of country living will continue to inform the Anglican view of God's work in Christ.

George Cambrensis

PREFACE

God's Country, the Gracewing Rural Life Anthologies, emerged from a sequence of conversations I enjoyed with Tim Cawkwell, Tony Hodgson and Mervyn Wilson, all leading members of the Rural Theology Association, a movement formed in the late 1970s to promote theological reflection on rural issues. Our shared idea in designing the series is to choose key themes with which rural theology must deal, like the country parson, country people, country places and rural spirituality. Our aim in exploring each theme is to treasure enduring images from the past and to nurture insights into the future. The present volume inaugurates the series.

I am grateful to my three colleagues for encouragement and help in shaping this volume and look forward to working with them in developing the *God's Country* series of rural life anthologies. My thanks are also due to Martin Marix-Evans for fostering the project during its infancy, to Tom Longford and Sheridan Swinson for editorial guidance and copyright clearance, to Richard Allen for the accompanying art work, to Kim Luckett and Kathleen Mills for help with preparing the manuscript, to many authors and publishers for permission to use their material, and to those special friends who allow me to raid their bookshelves whenever I visit their homes.

January 1989 Trinity College, Carmarthen.   Leslie J. Francis

INTRODUCTION

Recent years have witnessed radical changes in the structure of the rural church and fundamental reassessments in the deployment of rural clergy. To appreciate fully the significance of these discontinuities with the past for country folk and village life, it is necessary to examine the image of the central and influential role of the country parson in the recent past. In many cases the image has been exaggerated and romanticised through the conflation of memory and folk tradition with the richness of surviving clerical diaries and certain masterpieces of English literature. Nevertheless, it is precisely this image which breeds puzzlement in the minds of rural dwellers when they now fail to find their deep-seated ideas reflected in local reality. This helps to kindle rural antipathy towards the central church authorities to whom the villagers attribute the cause of change, and can make life difficult in unexpected ways for new-style country parsons coming up against old-style rural expectations.

Personally I first discovered the power of this image when my own ministry changed from an urban to a rural environment. Like so many Church of England priests, I was trained in the practical skills of ministry through working as a curate in a town. I became accustomed to serving in a church where there were specialist organisations for children and for young people, for men and for women, where there were house eucharist groups and study groups, where the parochial church council met once a month and was serviced by a range of subcommittees, where local lay initiative took charge of fund raising for major fabric repairs, where there was a relatively clear line drawn between people who came to church and those who did not, where the church music was competently arranged by a professional musician, and where three or four readers vied with two or three clergy to preach at the parish communion. In this town ecumenical relationships were important as Anglican, Methodist, Pentecostal, Roman Catholic, Salvation Army and United Reformed Church ministers met with each other in clergy groups and with the laity in the local council of churches. Yet the same ministers could walk incognito through the shopping centre on a Saturday morning and hardly recognise a familiar face.

In 1977, after the curacy, I moved into the countryside. Swapping the small town house for the large Victorian rural rectory was relatively easy, since kind parishioners came bearing curtains, carpets and cart loads of logs. Swapping the large town congregation for the small rural community required more adjustment. Fundamental ideas about conducting services, choosing music, preaching sermons, working with children, lay leadership, parochial church councils, ecumenical activity, and the basic relationship between church and society all needed to change, and to change radically and quickly.

In one sense, I recognised that in making the move to the country I had inherited a wealth of tradition and stability. This much was made plain by the brace of pheasants delivered to the door from the local estate of my patron so soon after I had moved into the rectory. In another sense, I recognised that I was part of a process of change and instability. Unlike the previous occupant of that rectory, I was priest-in-charge, not rector. Unlike the the previous occupant, I was non-stipendiary and working sixty miles away in London during much of every week, commuting alongside other new-comers to the village.

Since becoming a country parson, I have tried hard to listen to the voices of the rural past and to be sensitive to the potential for the rural future. Three of my earlier books have already documented part of this process: in *Rural Anglicanism* I employed the tools of social psychology to examine the strengths and weaknesses of the rural church today; in *Partnership in Rural Education* I employed the tools of educational research to trace the development of rural church schools and to explore their future; in *Making Contact* I documented stories of growth, development and hope in rural churches. Now in *The Country Parson* I assemble a collage of images celebrating the glories and the tragedies of the country parson's heritage, and displaying the range of contemporary visions for the country parson's future.

The country parson is a well documented figure, both in English literature and in social history. The difficulty in compiling the present anthology was not in finding good material, but in deciding which good material to leave out. The passages selected have been arranged thematically and not chronologically, in order to allow insights and reflections from different periods to interact with each other.

Chapter one begins with the ordination charge from *The Book of Common Prayer* (1662) and traces the experiences of those preparing for ordination, finding a rural living, beginning ministry in the countryside, settling in and staying for a lifetime. In chapter two, we meet the country parson at home in the parsonage, with his wife and family, and in a range of social circumstances from ostentatious affluence to extreme poverty. In chapter three, we meet the country parson at church, renovating the fabric, conducting Sunday services, preaching, officiating at baptisms, weddings and funerals. Chapter four shows the country parson about his work in the parish, visiting his parishioners in times of sickness and death and showing concern for their hardships, enjoying the hospitality of a good table, confronting dissenters, facing conflict, building schools and frequenting the inns. Chapter five shows the country parson engaging in a variety of other pursuits, farming his glebe, writing scholarly books, riding to hounds, becoming absorbed in bell-ringing or leading the village band.

Finally, chapter six builds on this rich and varied heritage to examine the direction in which the country parson might be developing in the future. It is abundantly clear that old patterns of the country parson are now rapidly disappearing, but it is not yet wholly clear what the new patterns of rural ministry should be. Chapter six displays the possibilities of multiple parish benefices, team and group ministries, lay leadership, local ministry, non-stipendiary ministry, ecumenical co-operation and the ministry of women, and concludes with the ordination charge from *The Alternative Service Book 1980*.

By bringing together images from the past and pointers for the future, my hope is that this anthology will prove to be of theoretical interest and practical benefit for today's rural clergy and for today's country dwellers. For the clergy, the images from the past will help to remind them of the traditions and deep-seated expectations which may be projected onto today's country parson. For the country dweller, the pointers to the future will help to alert them to the thinking and trends underlying the changes they observe and experience in today's rural ministry. Ultimately the challenge facing the rural church today is to know how best to embrace the future creatively, without forsaking and denying the potentially enduring strengths inherited from the past.

MOVING TO THE COUNTRY

1. MOVING TO THE COUNTRY

Considering Ordination

1.   We exhort you in the name of our Lord Jesus Christ, that you
     have in remembrance, into how high a dignity, and to how
weighty an office and charge ye are called: that is to say, to be
messengers, watchmen, and stewards of the Lord; to teach, and to
premonish, to feed and provide for the Lord's family; to seek for
Christ's sheep that are dispersed abroad, and for his children who
are in the midst of this naughty world, that they may be saved
through Christ for ever.

Have always therefore printed in your remembrance, how great a
treasure is committed to your charge. For they are the sheep of
Christ, which he bought with his death, and for whom he shed his
blood. The Church and Congregation whom you must serve, is his
spouse and his body. And if it shall happen the same Church, or any
member thereof, to take any hurt or hindrance by reason of your
negligence, ye know the greatness of the fault, and also the horrible
punishment that will ensure. Wherefore consider with yourselves
the end of your ministry towards the children of God, towards the
spouse and body of Christ; and see that you never cease your labour,
your care and diligence, until you have done all that lieth in you,
according to your bounden duty, to bring all such as are or shall be
committed to your charge, unto that agreement in the faith and
knowledge of God, and to that ripeness and perfectness of age in
Christ, that there be no place left among you, either for error in
religion, or for viciousness in life. . . .

We have good hope that you have well weighed and pondered these things with yourselves long before this time; and that you have clearly determined, by God's grace, to give yourselves wholly to this office, whereunto it hath pleased God to call you: so that, as much as lieth in you, you will apply yourselves wholly to this one thing, and draw all your cares and studies this way; and that you will continually pray to God the Father, by the mediation of our only Saviour Jesus Christ, for the heavenly assistance of the Holy Ghost; that, by daily reading and weighing of the Scriptures, ye may wax riper and stronger in your ministry; and that ye may so endeavour yourselves, from time to time, to sanctify the lives of you and yours, and to fashion them after the rule and doctrine of Christ, that ye may be wholesome and godly examples and patterns for the people to follow.

BOOK OF COMMON PRAYER (1662)

2.   There was a theological college at Melchester; Melchester was a quiet and soothing place, almost entirely ecclesiastical in its tone; a spot where worldly learning and intellectual smartness had no establishment; where the altruistic feeling that he did possess would perhaps be more highly estimated than a brilliancy which he did not.... To enter the Church in such an unscholarly way that he could not in any probability rise to a higher grade through all his career than that of the humble curate wearing his life out in an obscure village or city slum—that might have a touch of goodness and greatness in it; that might be true religion, and a purgatorial course worthy of being followed by a remorseful man....

As it would be necessary that he should continue for a time to work at his trade while reading up Divinity . . . what better course for him than to get employment at Melchester and pursue this plan of reading. . . ? He edged himself in by degrees. His first work was some carving at the cemetery on the hill; and ultimately he became engaged on the labour he most desired—the cathedral repairs, which were very extensive, the whole interior stonework having been overhauled, to be largely replaced by new.

It might be a labour of years to get it all done, and he had

16

confidence enough in his own skill with the mallet and chisel to feel that it would be a matter of choice with himself how long he would stay.

The lodgings he took near the Close Gate would not have disgraced a curate, the rent representing a higher percentage on his wages than merchanics of any sort usually care to pay. His combined bed and sitting-room was furnished with framed photographs of the rectories and deaneries at which his landlady had lived as trusted servant in her time. . . .

He found an ample supply of theological books in the city book-shops, and with these his studies were recommenced. . . . As a relaxation from the Fathers, and such stock works as Paley and Butler, he read Newman, Pusey, and many other modern lights. He hired a harmonium, set it up in his lodging, and practised chants thereon, single and double. . . .

He had, he verily believed, overcome all tendency to fly to liquor—which, indeed, he had never done from taste, but merely as an escape from intolerable misery of mind. Yet he perceived with despondency that, taken all round, he was a man of too many pas-sions to make a good clergyman; the utmost he could hope for was that in a life of constant internal warfare between flesh and spirit the former might not always be victorious.

THOMAS HARDY (1840—1926)

3. 'Ordained!' said Miss Crawford; 'what, are you to be a clergy-
    man. . . ? This is rather a surprise to me.'

'Why should it surprise you? You must suppose me designed for some profession, and might perceive that I am neither a lawyer, nor a soldier, nor a sailor.'

'Very true; but, in short, it had never occurred to me. And you know there is generally an uncle or a grandfather to leave a fortune to the second son.'

'A very praiseworthy practice,' said Edmund, 'but not quite universal. I am one of the exceptions, and being one, must do something for myself.'

'But why are you to be a clergyman? I thought that was always the lot of the youngest, where there were many to choose before him.'

'Do you think the church itself never chosen then?'

'*Never* is a black word. But yes, in the *never* of conversation which means *not very often*, I do think it. For what is to be done in the church? Men love to distinguish themselves, and in either of the other lines, distinction may be gained, but not in the church. A clergyman is nothing.'

'The *nothing* of conversation has its gradations, I hope, as well as the never. A clergyman cannot be high in state or fashion. He must not head mobs, or set the ton in dress. But I cannot call that situation nothing, which has the charge of all that is of the first importance to mankind, individually or collectively considered, temporally and eternally—which has the guardianship of religion and morals, and consequently of the manners which result from their influence. No one here can call the *office* nothing. . . .

'*You* assign greater consequence to the clergyman than one has been used to hear given, or than I can quite comprehend. One does not see much of this influence and importance in society, and how can it be acquired where they are so seldom seen themselves? How can two sermons a week, even supposing them worth hearing, supposing the preacher to have the sense to prefer Blair's to his own, do all that you speak of? govern the conduct and fashion the manners of a large congregation for the rest of the week? One scarcely sees a clergyman out of his pulpit.'

'You are speaking of London, *I* am speaking of the nation at large.'

'The metropolis, I imagine, is pretty fair sample of the rest.'

'Not, I should hope, of the proportion of virtue to vice throughout the kingdom. We do not look in great cities for our best morality. It is not there, that respectable people of any denomination can do most good; and it certainly is not there, that the influence of the clergy can be most felt. A fine preacher is followed and admired; but it is not in fine preaching only that a good clergyman will be useful in his parish and his neighbourhood, where the parish and neighbourhood are of a size capable of knowing his private character, and observing his general conduct, which in London can rarely be the case. . . . I wish I could convince Miss Crawford.'

'I do not think you ever will,' said she with an arch smile; 'I am just as much surprised now as I was at first that you should intend to take orders. You really are fit for something better. Come, do change your mind. It is not too late.... It is indolence Mr Bertram indeed. Indolence and love of ease—a want of all laudable ambition, of taste for good company, or of inclination to take the trouble of being agreeable, which makes men clergymen. A clergyman has nothing to do but to be slovenly and selfish—read the newspaper, watch the weather, and quarrel with his wife.

JANE AUSTEN (1775—1817)

4.   It was afternoon. All was as still in the Close as a cathedral-green can be between the Sunday services, and the incessant cawing of the rooks was the only sound. Joshua Halborough had finished his ascetic lunch, and had gone into the library, where he stood for a few moments looking out of the large window facing the green. He saw walking slowly across it a man in a fustian coat and a battered white hat with a much-ruffled nap, having upon his arm a tall gipsy-woman wearing long brass earrings. The man was staring quizzically at the west front of the cathedral, and Halborough recognized in him the form and features of his father. Who the woman was he knew not. Almost as soon as Joshua became conscious of these things, the sub-dean, who was also the principal of the Fountall Theological College, and of whom the young man stood in more awe than of the Bishop himself, emerged from the gate and entered a path across the Close. The pair met the dignitary, and to Joshua's horror his father turned and addressed the sub-dean.

What passed between them he could not tell. But as he stood in a cold sweat he saw his father place his hand familiarly on the sub-dean's shoulder; the shrinking response of the latter, and his quick withdrawal, told his feeling. The woman seemed to say nothing, but when the sub-dean had passed by they came on towards the college gate.

Halborough flew along the corridor and out at a side door, so as to intercept them before they could reach the front entrance, for which

19

they were making. He caught them behind a clump of laurel. . . .

In the evening he sat down and wrote a letter to his brother, in which, after stating what had happened, and expatiating upon this new disgrace in the gipsy wife, he propounded to plan for raising money sufficient to induce the couple to emigrate to Canada. 'It is our only chance,' he said. 'The case as it stands is maddening. For a successful painter, sculptor, musician, author, who takes society by storm, it is no drawback, it is sometimes even a romantic recommendation, to hail from outcasts and profligates. But for a clergyman of the Church of England! Cornelius, it is fatal! To succeed in the Church, people must believe in you, first of all, as a gentleman, secondly as a man of means, thirdly as a scholar, fourthly as a preacher, fifthly, perhaps, as a Christian,—but always first as a gentleman, with all their heart and soul and strength. I would have faced the fact of being a small machinist's son, and have taken my chance, if he'd been in any sense respectable and decent. The essence of Christianity is humility, and by the help of God I would have brazened it out. But this terrible vagabondage and disreputable connection! If he does not accept my terms and leave the country, it will extinguish us and kill me.'

THOMAS HARDY (1840—1928)

5.   Blest Order, which in power dost so excell,
That with th' one hand thou liftest to the sky,
And with the other throwest down to hell
In thy just censures; fain would I draw nigh,
Fain put thee on, exchanging my lay-sword
    For that of th' holy Word.

But thou art fire, sacred and hallow'd fire;
And I but earth and clay: should I presume
To wear thy habit, the severe attire
My slender compositions might consume.
I am both foul and brittle; much unfit
    To deal in holy Writ.

Yet have I often seen, by cunning hand
And force of fire, what curious things are made
Of wretched earth. Where once I scorn'd to stand,
That earth is fitted by the fire and trade
Of skilfull artists, for the boards of those
    Who make the bravest shows.

But since those great ones, be they ne're so great,
Come from the earth, from whence those vessels come;
So that at once both feeder, dish, and meat
Have one beginning and one finall summe:
I do not greatly wonder at the sight,
    If earth in earth delight.

But th' holy men of God such vessels are,
As serve him up, who all the world commands:
When God vouchsafeth to become our fare,
Their hands convey him, who conveys their hands.
O what pure things, most pure must those things be,
    Who bring my God to me!

Wherefore I dare not, I, put forth my hand
To hold the Ark, although it seem to shake
Through th' old sinnes and new doctrines of our land.
Onely, since God doth often vessels make
Of lowly matter for high uses meet,
    I throw me at his feet.

There will I lie, untill my Maker seek
For some mean stuffe whereon to show his skill:
Then is my time. The distance of the meek
Doth flatter power. Lest good come short of ill
In praising might, the poore do by submission
    What pride by opposition.

GEORGE HERBERT (1593—1633)

Finding a Living

6.   When young Mark Robarts was leaving college, his father might
      well declare that all men began to say all good things to him, and
to extol his fortune in that he had a son blessed with so excellent a
disposition. This father was a physician living at Exeter. . . .

Mark's first step forward in life had arisen from his having been
sent, while still very young, as a private pupil to the house of a clergyman, who was an old friend and intimate friend of his father's. This
clergyman had one other, and only one other, pupil—the young
Lord Lufton; and between the two boys, there had sprung up a close
alliance. While they were both so placed, Lady Lufton had visited
her son, and then invited young Robarts to pass his next holidays at
Framley Court. This visit was made; and it ended in Mark going back
to Exeter with a letter full of praise from the widowed peeress. She
had been delighted, she said, in having such a companion for her
son, and expressed a hope that the boys might remain together
during the course of their education. . . . When, therefore, the
young lord was sent to Harrow, Mark Robarts went there also. . . .
And then the lads went together to Oxford, and here Mark's good
fortune followed him. . . .

Then came the question of a profession for this young Hyperion,
and on this subject, Dr Robarts was invited himself to go over to
Framley Court to discuss the matter with Lady Lufton. Dr Robarts
returned with a very strong conception that the Church was the
profession best suited to his son.

Lady Lufton had not sent for Dr Robarts all the way from Exeter
for nothing. The living of Framley was in the gift of the Lufton family,
and the next presentation would be in Lady Lufton's hands, if it
should fall vacant before the young lord was twenty-five years of
age, and in the young lord's hands if it should fall afterwards. But the
mother and the heir consented to give a joint promise to Dr Robarts.
Now, as the present incumbent was over seventy, and as the living
was worth £900 a year, there could be no doubt as to the eligibility of
the clerical profession. And I must further say, that the dowager and
the doctor were justified in their choice by the life and principles of

the young man—as far as any father can be justified in choosing such a profession for his son, and as far as any lay impropriator can be justified in making such a promise. . . .

Lady Lufton herself was a woman who thought much on religious matters, and would by no means have been disposed to place any one in a living, merely because such a one had been her son's friend. Her tendencies were High Church, and she was enabled to perceive that those of young Mark Robarts ran in the same direction. She was very desirous that her son should make an associate of his clergyman, and by this step she would insure, at any rate, that. She was anxious that the parish vicar should be one with whom she could herself fully co-operate, and was perhaps unconsciously wishful that he might in some measure be subject to her influence. Should she appoint an elder man, this might probably not be the case to the same extent; and should her son have the gift, it might probably not be the case at all. And, therefore, it was resolved that the living should be given to young Robarts.

He took his degree—not with any brilliancy, but quite in the manner that his father desired; he then travelled for eight or ten months with Lord Lufton and a college don, and almost immediately after his return home was ordained.

The living of Framley is in the diocese of Barchester; and, seeing what were Mark's hopes with reference to that diocese, it was by no means difficult to get him a curacy within it. But this curacy he was not allowed long to fill. He had not been in it above a twelvemonth, when poor old Dr Stopford, the then vicar of Framley, was gathered to his fathers, and the full fruition of his rich hopes fell upon his shoulders.

ANTHONY TROLLOPE (1815—1882)

7. Parson Bate left London in 1782 and bought the advowson of Bradwell-on-Sea for £1,500. When he first came to the village it was a desolate, dirty, plague-ridden spot with inadequate drainage and no roads. The absentee rector had allowed both church and rectory to crumble into ruins. Mr Bate changed all that. Over the next fif-

teen years he spent £30,000 of his own money building roads, improving drainage and repairing the church, the rectory and many of the cottages. He lived at the rectory himself and acted as curate.

In 1784 Mr Bate inherited a fortune from a relative and, in compliance with the will, assumed the additional name of Dudley....

In 1797 the incumbent of Bradwell died and Bate-Dudley presented himself to the living. The Bishop of London refused to institute him, however, believing that he was guilty of simony. The matter was taken to court, but by the time a compromise had been reached it was discovered that the right of presentation had passed to the Crown and that Mr Gamble, Chaplain-General of the Army, had been appointed. It seemed very hard that Bate-Dudley should receive nothing after all he had done for Bradwell, and many influential people pleaded with the Government on his behalf. Nothing came of their intercession, and the parson obtained no pecuniary compensation.

ALISON BARNES (1947—   )

8.   Mr Smith did not enter the ministry of the Church of England on account of any great religious conviction or sense of vocation.... As a scholar of Eton and of King's College, Cambridge, with a fine voice and a good presence ..., he entered an Oxford theological college, and as soon as he was ordained priest he accepted an invitation to return to King's College as chaplain. There he entertained undergraduates to Madeira, and intoned the chapel services with an impeccable sense of pitch and an exquisite appreciation of the cadences of Elizabethan English. Then after a few years it happened, in the Church of England way, that one evening the Provost took him aside after a college feast and said, 'My dear Smith, we have fortuitously rather a good living vacant in Lincolnshire. Or perhaps fortuitously is not the word, for they say, if I recall correctly, that the late incumbent killed himself. The living is not by any means one of the recognized steps on the ladder, or whatever one ascends in the Anglican Church; but think about it, Smith, think about it!

Rowlands will give you the precise details—it may be in Norfolk; but I am credibly informed that we have a living vacant somewhere. Of course, Smith, we should be sorry to lose you because you don't mumble, but I thought I ought to tell you. Think about it, my dear Smith. Please do.'

Smith did not think seriously about it at all, and it was only out of idle curiosity he went to see a Lincolnshire parish with a stipend of two thousand pounds a year and the scene of a clerical suicide. For the first reason alone it was a comparative rarity. The visit was his undoing, for the widow of the late incumbent was still, by arrangement with the churchwardens, living in the Rectory as caretaker, and she had retained four of the servants, amongst whom was a rather beautiful seventeen-year-old girl called Bridget Atkinson, of a Hedingham family distantly related to mine. From the age of fourteen Smith had been troubled by the flesh but had been too fearful and shy to make carnal overtures to any woman, until in his second year at Cambridge he had joined a party of rich young men who regularly bribed their bedmakers not to report them absent when they went off by train for a night in London. There Smith quenched temporarily his sensual thirst in a discreet and expensive brothel where the girls were young. . . .

Smith was a bachelor when the widow invited him to stay the night at Hedingham Rectory, and Bridget Atkinson was the housemaid who preceded him up the winding oak staircase to show him his room. He could only be reminded of other girls, no more lovely, who had walked before him with swinging hips and backward smiling glances along other corridors leading to other rooms with large beds. Bridget stayed to light his fire, to unpack his bag, and to pour out water from the ewer into his wash-bowl, while he sat on the bed watching every movement she made. As she came to turn down the sheets he rose to his feet and asked, much too quietly, 'If I became the rector here, would you stay and work for me?' Bridget turned quickly and glanced at him. Village girls seldom reached the age of seventeen in innocence, and Smith's eyes had, though he didn't know it, long surrendered their chastity to his experience. Perhaps at that moment Bridget did not conclude explicitly what working for the Reverend Mr Smith might involve, but she was at least conscious that her answer was of greater importance to the questioner than the mere availability of a housemaid in a locality where there was no shortage. She hesitated and Smith sensed that he had been too precipitate. 'Of course,' he added, 'I should want to employ the four of you. I have no wife to arrange servants for me and I suppose you all know how to run the place.' 'Oh yes, sir,' replied Bridget, seeing an advantage for her fellow servants, 'and I shall be pleased to stay if the others will.' It happened that the others were also pleased to work for him, so Smith resigned his chaplaincy and accepted the gift of a cure of souls, with substantial temporalities, from the hands of the Provost and Fellows of King's College, Cambridge, for no better reason than that he ached to employ Bridget Atkinson as his housemaid.

GEOFFREY ROBINSON (1917 —   )

Beginning Ministry

9. He is likely to find himself at the beginning of his ministry in a
    small and inconspicuous parish, which may seem to present
scant opportunity for the exercise of his powers. In this he is
mistaken, for the smallest parish presents opportunities beyond the
powers of those most richly endowed. He could labour there all his
life and perform a work of vast significance . . . . To it he will apply
himself with all his God-given powers and exercise all the talents he
possesses. His congregation may be small and unlearned, but he will
prepare his sermons with the utmost care and fashion them
according to the needs of his people. The funds may be limited; all
the more he will seek to have them used to the best advantage. The
equipment may be poor; he will study how it may be improved. The
parish may be composed of only a few hundred souls; he will
remember that each one of these has its need of sacramental grace.
The children may be few, yet not one of them may grow beyond all
human reckoning in character and influence. In a word, he idealizes
the whole situation, sees in it the possibilities of spiritual romance,
and devotes to it every capacity of mind and soul.

Thus he learns the essential technique of a spiritual ministry.
Indeed there is a sense in which 'pastoral care' can be learned not in
a school of theology but only in the care of a parish. He acquires skills
in the use of his tools; in methods of administration; in the ways of
the religious training of the young; in parish visitation. The smallest
parish offers a minister an invaluable opportunity of learning his
trade. And to the degree to which he devotes himself
wholeheartedly and with interest and imagination to his work, does
he acquire competency and efficiency. He becomes disciplined in
every aspect of his task.

RAYMOND CALKINS (1869 —   )

10. On the following Sunday Mr Arabin was to read himself in at
     his new church. It was agreed at the rectory that the
archdeacon should go over with him and assist at the reading-
desk. . . .

On the Sunday morning the archdeacon with his sister-in-law and Mr Arabin drove over to Ullathorne, as had been arranged. On their way thither the new vicar declared himself to be considerably disturbed in his mind at the idea of thus facing his parishioners for the first time. He had, he said, been always subject to *mauvaise honte* and an annoying degree of bashfulness, which often unfitted him for any work of a novel description; and now he felt this so strongly that he feared he should acquit himself badly in St Ewold's reading-desk. He knew, he said, that those sharp little eyes of Miss Thorne would be on him, and that they would not approve. All this the archdeacon greatly ridiculed. He himself knew not, and had never known, what it was to be shy. . . .

Mr Arabin read the lessons and preached. It was enough to put a man a little out, let him have been ever so used to pulpit reading, to see the knowing way in which the farmers cocked their ears, and set about a mental criticism as to whether their new minister did or did not fall short of the excellence of him who had lately departed from them. A mental and silent criticism it was for the existing moment, but soon to be made public among the elders of St Ewold's over the green graves of their children and forefathers. The excellence, how-ever, of poor old Mr Goodenough had not been wonderful, and there were few there who did not deem that Mr Arabin did his work sufficiently well, in spite of the slightly nervous affection which at first impeded him, and which nearly drove the archdeacon beside him-self.

Anthony Trollope (1815—1882)

11.   It was the sheerest bad luck that the new vicar of Beckindale, the Reverend William Hockley, came upon them first thing next morning. A keen keep-fit enthusiast, Hockley was out for his early morning jog, and took his way out from the vicarage past the school along Demdyke Row, intending to run out past the cricket field.

He saw Joe Sugden come out of a door in the middle of the row of cottages. Joe was in a hurry; it was time to be in the mistle. The two of

28

them almost collided on the footpath outside the gate. 'Morning Joe,' said the vicar, recalling his name from what Annie Sugden had said about the young man who was to collect her from a parish meeting.

'Morning, vicar,' said Joe and rushed on.

There was a young woman in a dressing-gown—or perhaps it was an overall—in the doorway. 'Morning, Mrs Sugden,' carolled Hockley, and jogged on to the end of the row, through the alley to the cricket pitch, and round the perimeter. He was passing the score-board when a thought occurred that made him flush to the roots of his hair. Annie Sugden had said that her son Joe was on his own at the present time, awaiting a divorce from his wife Christine.

So who was the young woman in the doorway?

Kathy had turned back into the house after the vicar's greeting, divided between ironic mirth and embarrassment. She drew the overall about her more closely.

LEE MACKENZIE (1928 —   )

Settling In

12.   Towards the end of my third year at Tiverton, I received an invitation . . . to accept the 'living' of two parishes . . . at Bradford and Thornbury. . . . The parishes had been vacant for about a year, several priests having been to look at them, but in each case they had turned down the bishop's offer because they thought the rectory at Bradford was too large.

This house was a beautiful example of Elizabethan architecture. It had nine bedrooms and an 'alms-hole' of that time. This was a tiny room from which the priest distributed the alms to the poor of the parish. The winding staircase was of polished oak, with the arms of Exeter cathedral and bishop's mitres carved in various places. A large window above the staircase was of stained glass, depicting saints and their crowns. There were also two large lawns, a garden and four acres of glebeland, with the most beautiful avenue of beech trees. . . .

After some two years at Bradford and Thornbury, Dorothy and I began to feel that we were not being stretched to our full capacity, and that there were areas in our lives that needed to be looked at. The first of these was our house with its nine bedrooms—only two of which were in use, so we decided to give holidays to deprived children. An organisation in Bristol undertook to cover the cost of their rail fares, and we did the best we could to give them an experience to remember.

All the children, who had never before had a holiday, came from very poor families. I remember one little boy who arrived wearing a jacket that was obviously his father's, with the sleeves reaching below his fingertips. For these little ones a visit to the seaside was something out of this world; one little lad stood on the cliff-top and gasped, 'My, what a lot of water.' I doubt if that old rectory had heard such shrieks of laughter echoing through its corridors for many a long year. We had our moments of frustration when these children, who had never before been outside their city boundaries, began to spread their wings during the first few days of their visit. One never knew what mischief they would be doing next—all of which was a great trial to Bill, because it was generally his animals with which they became involved. These children obviously enjoyed their holidays, but this was more than matched by the joy that was ours in seeing those little lives unfolding in the fresh air and the freedom of the countryside—something we took for granted.

After a while we felt that our home was still not being used to its fullest capacity, so we decided to foster children on a temporary basis. This would cover the whole year instead of just holiday times. Little did we think that when little Mark came to us he would be the first of forty-five who would share our home down the years. Mark's mum wished to do nursing training, and having no one to care for him during that time, he stayed with us for three years. Today he is a massive six-footer, but still calls us 'my other gran and grandad'.

F. PENNINGTON (1911—   )

13.   One day goes by, and then the next. . . . How empty they seem! I just get to the end of my day's work, but I always put off till to-morrow the carrying out of the little plan I had in mind. Obviously I lack method. And I spend so much time out on the road. My nearest boundary is a distance of three good kilometres—the other, five. My bicycle is not much help since I can't possibly ride uphill, especially on an empty stomach, without the most horrible pains. . . . Yet this parish looks so small on the map! When I think how it takes a teacher well into the second term to get to know a class of thirty or forty children of the same age and type, brought up and educated alike—and even then he won't always understand each one separately. . . I feel that my life, all the sap of my life will flow to waste in sand.

G. BERNANOS (1888—1948)

14.   Within his curtain of trees below church and village, my father had difficulty enough in the beginning. He was an East Anglian, not a Cornishman. He was a stranger who had to be teased and tested. His orchard was robbed, coal was taken from the vast cel-

lar. . . . But he stayed; and staying makes all the difference. The church in its old wisdom made the parson's living his freehold. The parson entered upon his living, and then shifting him, if he did no heinous villainy, was. . .like trying to shift Helvellyn. If this meant security for the bad priest, it meant security as well for the good, it gave the good man authority and the will, and ability, to resist. Stay, and you are likely to be accepted. My father was accepted, liked, and loved, I think, before the end; for at least he came from a line of parsons used, if in a different society and county, to the peculiarities of the country parish. . . . He was no retired electrician who had felt a call; he was no worn-out urban or suburban cleric, who had retired like an old cab horse to a small pasture. His parishioners could feel that he possessed a knowledge of the world outside the parish; and not only at church, at christenings, marryings and buryings, was he useful to them. And he became well rooted in Pelynt. He had seven children born in the vicarage, christened in the church and brought up among the farms and cottages.

GEOFFREY GRIGSON (1905—1985)

15.   By ten o'clock in the morning Hilary had already done what many people would have considered quite a good day's work. He got up always at six, had his tepid bath, shaved and dressed . . . went downstairs to his study and prayed and meditated for an hour. At seven forty-five he crossed the garden and the lane to the small grey church half hidden among the great churchyard yews, and struggled into his surplice and stole in the vestry while Thomas Trickup the verger, who was also the village butcher, and a very excellent churchman besides, tolled the bell. At eight Hilary said Mass, his week-day congregation consisting, winter and summer alike, of Trickup, Miss Marble from Lavender Cottage, Margaret— when she could get away, and a robin. On Sundays he had quite a large congregation, for he had been vicar of Fairhaven for over twenty years and had brought it up very firmly in the way it should go, but it would take him another twenty years, if he lived as long, to persuade any but the faithful four to come to church on a week-day. Yet

32

Fairhaven liked to hear the bell tolling out every morning . . . . The ungodly, rousing from sleep, set their watches by this bell, and the godly, whilst also setting their watches, remembered that at this hour Hilary was praying for them. They were glad of that.

ELIZABETH GOUDGE (1900—1984)

CHURCH

Staying in the Country

16. I arrived in the village immediately after the last war and so I have seen the 'revolution'—I think you can call it that. I came from the Welsh valleys, where my father was also a clergyman, and where the industrial dereliction of the 1930s sprawled for as far as one could see, to a part of Suffolk where the old feudal system was dying hard.... I have been very happy here and what I have to say about the people mustn't be taken for negative criticism. I am a Celt and different to them.... The church was abysmally dull when I came and there was no parish communion. No warmth or feeling. It was very noticeable after Wales.

I came to live in friendship and understanding with most of the inhabitants but I found that to talk on any deep level about their Christianity was intensely difficult—even when death was round the corner! It could have been me, of course! I don't think that the ordinary villager, who is linked to deeper propitiatory practices in the fields than he is aware of, has either the energy or feels the need to inquire what the Church is all about....

One of my most difficult tasks has been to persuade little groups of people to get together and, in a very simple and friendly way, to discuss the meaning of the Faith. But no one would come to a meeting if he thought he had to say something. When they have said something, one often finds that it is something quite irrelevant to what is being discussed. Religion has a lot to do with where their families and ancestors are buried. They spend hours tending graves and they are also very concerned about the state of the churchyard. Television is now breaking down their silences. They are getting accustomed to the idea of dialogue. The old villager was very different: he accepted or rejected but he said nothing. There was no debate, or argument, as he called it. One discovered saints, of course, people of prayer and worship, men of profound simplicity and to whose natural conception of the divine one could neither add nor subtract a thing. But generally speaking, the God of the Suffolk countryman tended to live outside the church, which was a building near the graves, and thus holy. It was all very vague. One could never get really near to them where such matters were concerned, as one could get near to the Celt.

I remember an example of the importance attached to church burial. When old Thrussel died, his widow came to me and said that he wished to be buried in the churchyard. I was very surprised to hear this because he'd been a Strict Baptist all his life and had been far from friendly towards the church. The Baptists, of course, have got their own burial ground behind the chapel. Why couldn't he be buried there? 'He fancied the churchyard,' stated his wife—'that bit up by the top there.' The penny now dropped. I recalled great battles with Mr Thrussel about a scrap of land which we had had to take in order to extend the churchyard. He had fought us all along the line but lost. Now he was getting his own back by being buried, as he believed, on his own farm! I always liked this old man. He and his family were all out of the common run, vital and clever. In the early days they had to struggle in a way you never see now. It made him tough and acquisitive. Whatever he gained he held. Bitterly. He was like the rest of the working farmers here. They didn't see this attitude as meanness but as strength. Life had taught Mr Thrussel to hang on tight!

I am not really close to them. When I first came they said, 'You'll have to winter us and summer us, sir', and twenty years later I'm still doing this, if the truth be known.

RONALD BLYTHE (1922—   )

17.   The countrey parson is a lover of old customes, if they be good and harmlesse; and the rather because countrey people are much addicted to them, so that to favour them therein is to win their hearts, and to oppose them therein is to deject them. If there be any ill in the custome that may be severed from the good, he pares the apple, and gives them the clean to feed on. Particularly he loves procession, and maintains it, because there are contained therein 4 manifest advantages: first, a blessing of God for the fruits of the field; secondly, justice in the preservation of bounds; thirdly, charity in loving walking and neighbourly accompanying one another, with

36

reconciling of differences at that time, if there be any; fourthly, mercy in releeving the poor by a liberall distribution and largesse, which at that time is or ought to be used. Wherefore he exacts of all to bee present at the perambulation, and those that withdraw and sever themselves from it he mislikes, and reproves as uncharitable and unneighbourly; and if they will not reforme, presents them. Nay, he is so farre from condemning such assemblies, that he rather procures them to be often, as knowing that absence breeds strangeness, but presence love.

GEORGE HERBERT (1593—1633)

18.   As a country vicar my father was completely identified with the life and work of his parishioners. He would turn out in the hay-field or harvest-field day after day to help some belated farmer to get up his crop; he would mow the churchyard with a scythe, assist his sexton in digging a grave; and, clad as he often was in the oldest of clothes he was once given threepence for minding a bicycle while a visitor looked over the church, while on another occasion he arrived home grinning, having earned sixpence by conducting a fellow-parson and some friends round it. A remarkably intelligent man for my station in life he declared me to be, he chuckled.

J.E. LINNELL (1842—1919)

19.   Henry Savage was sitting on an old oak seat on the terrace. Behind him, against the wall of the house, a fountain of forsythia sprayed up. They made an odd contrast: this springing gold with the sunshine upon it and this thin rusty-black man. A black wide-awake hat had been put down on the stone by his feet, so I saw his face in that first glance. His untidy beard and his hair were iron-grey. He was looking over the countryside with hooded eyes, set deep on either side of a massive eagle-beak of a nose. His clothes were black and careless, and he wore a parson's collar. He was leaning forward with both hands clasped on the knob of a blackthorn stick. . . .

37

average Norfolk labourer? I have worked and worked hard for nearly sixty years amongst them and I am no nearer to them—generally speaking—than I ever was. We are good friends—they touch their caps to me and all that—but oh! the gulf between us makes my heart shrivel up. The conversation is generally my own ideas, just altered a bit and handed back. . . .'

His church was 'my great effort for the souls of my people,' but 'my choir is now reduced from five men to three, of whom one is occupied on Sunday mornings with horses and bullocks (I as a farmer for forty years know it all) and the other two that are left are mightily afraid of being left alone. And if the church is likely to be nearly empty the few won't come. The herd instinct is always on top. . . .'

So hard. After mentioning to one of his parishioners one day that he had been rector for sixty years he got the reply 'I reckon it's about time you retired.' It was kindly meant. The Norfolk way of saying 'you've earned a rest.' Did his parishioners realize that in these last and most difficult years their faithful old rector was tackling by far the hardest job he had ever tackled, against the black despair and the feeling that the whole of his long life and ministry had been a failure—'and nothing fails like failure.' I am sure they never did. It would not have occurred to them. 'He keep a duin' and they admired him for it, though they would never say it or give the slightest intimation of it.

CHARLES LINNELL

Henry Savage got up and knocked out his pipe. 'Well,' he said, 'I don't envy you. Places like this are doomed.... It's a contracting age. Everything is diminishing: men's houses, men's hearts and men's souls. Well, thank God he'll soon be taking me out of it all. I shall be ninety next month.'

I was amazed. I should have given him no more than seventy years. He looked and spoke like a man in lean vigour of body and mind. I think his few remarks had left me looking crestfallen, for he laid a bony hand on my shoulder.... 'Come along then,' he said. 'There are two miles to walk.'

We set off southward, in the direction of the sea. Mr Savage was a cross-country walker. Here and there we were in a lane, but most of the time we were walking through pastures and spinneys.... 'I like to do my five or six miles a day, rain or shine,' he said. 'I've been doing it now for sixty-five years and established a sort of momentum. Yes. It was in this month—in March—that I came to the vicarage sixty-five years ago. I was an aspiring young man—Rugby—Balliol. I'd just married. Winchester was my lowest ambition. Canterbury did not seem remote. Well, glory be to God—I've been spared that. It's a bit late now even for Truro.'

HOWARD SPRING (1889—1965)

20. The fact that Canon Marcon died in the same room in which he had been born at Edgefield Rectory, the parish of which he had been rector in succession to his father, would not have appeared so remarkable at any time in the seventeenth, eighteenth or nineteenth centuries as it did at the time of his death in 1937. In 1850, the year of his birth, and in 1875, the year of his institution to Edgefield, church and parish remained in almost every respect exactly the same as they had done for centuries....

In the last year or two of his life Canon Marcon communicated to the Revd P.S. Raby, Rector of Ingworth and a new-comer to the district, some revealing, but at the same time very saddening, reflections about his work.

'What do you think,' he wrote on January 10th, 1934, 'of the

RELAXING AT HOME

2. AT HOME

Courtship

21.   'Believe me, my dear Miss Elizabeth. . ., that I have your respected mother's permission for this address. You can hardly doubt the purport of my discourse, however your natural delicacy may lead you to dissemble; my attentions have been too marked to be mistaken. Almost as soon as I entered the house, I singled you out as the companion of my future life. But before I am run away with by my feelings on this subject, perhaps it would be advisable for me to state my reasons for marrying—and moreover for coming into Hertfordshire with the design of selecting a wife, as I certainly did.'

The idea of Mr Collins, with all his solemn composure, being run away with by his feelings, made Elizabeth so near laughing that she could not use the short pause he allowed in any attempt to stop him farther, and he continued:

'My reasons for marrying are, first, that I think it a right thing for every clergyman in easy circumstances (like myself) to set the example of matrimony in his parish. Secondly, that I am convinced it will add very greatly to my happiness; and thirdly, which perhaps I ought to have mentioned earlier, that it is the particular advice and recommendation of the very noble lady whom I have the honour of calling patroness. Twice has she condescended to give me her opinion (unasked too!) on this subject; and it was but the very Saturday night before I left Hunsford—between our pools at quadrille, while Mrs Jenkins was arranging Miss De Bourgh's footstall—that she said, 'Mr Collins, you must marry. A clergyman like you must marry. Choose properly, choose a gentlewoman, for *my* sake; and for your *own*; let her be an active, useful sort of person, not brought up high, but able to make a small income go a good way. . .'. Thus much for my general intention in favour of matrimony; it remains to be told why my views were directed to Longbourne instead of my own neighbourhood, where, I assure you, there are many amiable young women. But the fact is, that being, as I am, to inherit this estate after the death of your honoured father, (who, however, may live many years longer,) I could not satisfy myself without resolving to choose a wife from among his daughters, that the loss to them might be as little as possible, when the melancholy event takes place—which, however, as I have already said, may not be for several years. This has been my motive, my fair cousin, and I flatter myself it will not sink me in your esteem. And now nothing remains for me but to assure you in the most animated language of the violence of my affection. . .'.

It was absolutely necessary to interrupt him now.

'You are too hasty, sir,' she cried. 'You forget that I have made no answer. Let me do it without further loss of time. Accept my thanks for the compliment you are paying me. I am very sensible of the honour of your proposals, but it is impossible for me to do otherwise than decline them.'

JANE AUSTEN (1775—1817)

22. The Rev. Caleb Oriel delighted in lecterns and credence-tables, in services at dark hours of winter mornings when no one would attend, in high waistcoats and narrow white neckties, in chanted services and intoned prayers, and in all the paraphernalia of Anglican formalities which have given such offence to those of our brethren who live in daily fear of the scarlet lady. Many of his friends declared that Mr Oriel would sooner or later deliver himself over body and soul to that lady; but there was no need to fear for him: for though sufficiently enthusiastic to get out of bed at five a.m. on winter mornings—he did so, at least, all through his first winter at

42

Greshamsbury—he was not made of that stuff which is necessary for a stanch, burning, self-denying convert. . . .

Mr Oriel soon became popular. He was a dark-haired, good-looking man, of polished manners, agreeable in society, not given to monkish austerities—except in the matter of Fridays—nor yet to the low-church severity of demeanour. He was thoroughly a gentleman, good-humoured, inoffensive, and sociable. But he had one fault: he was not a marrying man. . . .

There were around Greshamsbury very many unmarried ladies—I believe there generally are so round most such villages. From the great house he did not receive much annoyance. Beatrice was then only just on the verge of being brought out, and was not perhaps inclined to think very much of a young clergyman; and Augusta certainly intended to fly at higher game. But there were the Miss Athelings, the daughters of a neighbouring clergyman, who were ready to go all lengths with him in high-church matters, except as to that one tremendously papal step of celibacy; and the two Miss Hesterwells, of Hesterwell Park, the younger of whom boldly declared her purpose of civilising the savage; and Mrs Opie Green, a very pretty widow, with a very pretty jointure, who lived in a very pretty house about a mile from Greshamsbury. . . .

And then there was Miss Gushing,—a young thing. Miss Gushing had a great advantage over the other competitors for the civilisation of Mr Oriel, namely, in this—that she was able to attend his morning services. If Mr Oriel was to be reached in any way, it was probable that he might be reached in this way. If anything could civilise him, this would do it. Therefore, the young thing, through all one long, tedious winter, tore herself from her warm bed, and was to be seen— no, not seen, but heard—entering Mr Oriel's church at six o'clock. With indefatigable assiduity the responses were made, uttered from under a close bonnet, and out of a dark corner, in an enthusiastically feminine voice, through the whole winter.

Nor did Miss Gushing altogether fail in her object. When a clergyman's daily audience consists of but one person, and that person is a young lady, it is hardly possible that he should not become personally intimate with her; hardly possible that he should not be in some measure grateful. Miss Gushing's responses came from her with such fervour, and she begged for ghostly advice with such eager longing to have her scruples satisfied, that Mr Oriel had nothing for it but give way to a certain amount of civilisation.

By degrees it came to pass that Miss Gushing could never get her final prayer said, her shawl and boa adjusted, and stow away her nice new prayer-book with the red letters inside, and the cross on the back, till Mr Oriel had been into his vestry and got rid of his surplice. And then they met at the church-porch, and naturally walked together till Mr Oriel's cruel gateway separated them. . . .

Then Miss Gushing took to fasting on Fridays, and made some futile attempts to induce her priest to give her the comfort of confessional absolution. But, unfortunately, the zeal of the master waxed cool as that of the pupil waxed hot; and, at last, when the young thing returned to Greshamsbury from an autumn excursion which she had made with Mrs Umbleby to Weston-super-Mare, she found that the delicious morning services had died a natural death. Miss Gushing did not on that account give up the game, but she was bound to fight with no particular advantage in her favour.

ANTHONY TROLLOPE (1815—1882)

23.   At the time of which I am speaking (said Mr Mulliner) my nephew Augustine was a curate, and very young and extremely pale. . . . The personality of his immediate superior did little or nothing to help him to overcome his native diffidence. The Rev. Stanley Brandon was a huge and sinewy man of violent temper, whose red face and glittering eyes might well have intimidated the toughest curate. . . . And yet it was to the daughter of this formidable man that Augustine Mulliner had permitted himself to lose his heart. Truly, Cupid makes heroes of us all.

Jane was a very nice girl, and just as fond of Augustine as he was of her. But, as each lacked the nerve to go to the girl's father and put him abreast of the position of affairs, they were forced to meet surreptitiously. This jarred upon Augustine who, like all the Mulliners, loved the truth and hated any form of deception. And one

44

evening, as they paced beside the laurels at the bottom of the vicarage garden, he rebelled.

'My dearest,' said Augustine, 'I can no longer brook this secrecy. I shall go into the house immediately and ask your father for your hand.'

Jane paled and clung to his arm. She knew so well that it was not her hand but her father's foot which he would receive if he carried out this mad scheme.

'No, no, Augustine! You must not!'

'But, darling, it is the only straightforward course.'

'But not tonight. I beg you, not tonight.'

'Why not?'

'Because father is in a very bad temper. He has just had a letter from the bishop, rebuking him for wearing too many orphreys on his chasuble, and it has upset him terribly. You see, he and the bishop were at school together, and father can never forget it. He said at dinner that if old Boko Bickerton thought he was going to order him about he would jolly well show him.'

'And the bishop comes here tomorrow for the Confirmation services!' gasped Augustine.

'Yes. And I'm afraid they will quarrel. It's such a pity father hasn't some other bishop over him. He always remembers that he once hit this one in the eye for pouring ink on his collar, and this lowers his respect for his spiritual authority. So you won't go in and tell him tonight, will you?'

'I will not,' Augustine assured her with a slight shiver.

'And you will be sure to put your feet in hot mustard and water when you get home? The dew has made the grass so wet.'

'I will indeed, dearest.'

'You are not strong, you know.'

'No, I am not strong. . . . Good night, Jane.'

'Good night, Augustine.'

The lovers parted. Jane slipped back into the vicarage, and Augustine made his way to his cosy rooms in the High Street.

P.G. WODEHOUSE (1881—1975)

Marriage

24.   The temporal concerns of our family were chiefly committed
      to my wife's management; as to the spiritual, I took them
entirely under my own direction. . . .

Matrimony was always one of my favourite topics, and I wrote
several sermons to prove its happiness; but there was a peculiar
tenet which I made a point of supporting: for I maintained, with
Whiston, that it was unlawful for a priest of the Church of England,
after the death of his first wife, to take a second; or, to express it in one
word, I valued myself upon being a strict monogamist.

I was early initiated into this important dispute, on which so many
laborious volumes have been written. I published some tracts upon
the subject myself, which, as they never sold, I have the consolation
of thinking were read only by the happy *few*. Some of my friends
called this my weak side; but, alas! they had not, like me, made it the
subject of long contemplation. The more I reflected upon it, the
more important it appeared. I even went a step beyond Whiston in
displaying my principles: as he had engraven upon his wife's tomb
that she was the *only* wife of William Whiston; so I wrote a similar
epitaph for my wife, though still living, in which I extolled her
prudence, economy, and obedience till death; and, having got it
copied fair, with an elegant frame, it was placed over the chimney-
piece, where it answered several very useful purposes. It
admonished my wife of her duty to me, and my fidelity to her; it
inspired her with a passion for fame, and consequently put her in
mind of her end.

It was thus, perhaps, from hearing marriage so often
recommended, that my eldest son, just upon leaving college, fixed
his affections upon the daughter of a neighbouring clergyman, who
was a dignitary in the Church, and in circumstances to give her a
large fortune.

OLIVER GOLDSMITH (1728—1774)

25.   I have often thought that the Church of Rome does wisely in
      not allowing her priests to marry. Certainly it is a matter of com-
mon observation in England that the sons of clergymen are frequently unsatisfactory. The explanation is very simple. . . .

The clergyman is expected to be a kind of human Sunday. Things
must not be done in him which are venial in the week-day classes. He
is paid for this business of leading a stricter life than other people. It is
his *raison d'être*. If his parishioners feel that he does this, they
approve of him, for they look upon him as their own contribution
towards what they deem a holy life. This is why the clergyman is so
often called a vicar—he being the person whose vicarious goodness
is to stand for that of those entrusted to his charge. But his home is his
castle as much as that of any other Englishman, and with him, as with
others, unnatural tension in public is followed by exhaustion when
tension is no longer necessary. His children are the most
defenceless things he can reach, and it is on them in nine cases out of
ten that he will relieve his mind.

SAMUEL BUTLER (1835—1902)

26.   *Miss Prism*. You are too much alone, dear Dr Chasuble. You
      should get married. A misanthrope I can understand—a
womanthrope, never!

Dr Chasuble. Believe me, I do not deserve so neologistic a phrase.
The precept as well as the practice of the Primitive Church was distinctly against matrimony.

Miss Prism. That is obviously the reason why the Primitive Church
has not lasted up to the present day. And you do not seem to realise,
dear Doctor, that by persistently remaining single, a man converts
himself into a permanent public temptation. Men should be more
careful; this very celibacy leads weaker vessels astray.

Dr Chasuble. But is a man not equally attractive when married?

Miss Prism. No married man is ever attractive except to his wife.

Dr Chasuble. And often, I've been told, not even to her.

OSCAR WILDE (1856—1900)

27. The earliest set of letters were two bundles tied together, and ticketed, 'Letters interchanged between my ever-honoured father and my dearly-beloved mother, prior to their marriage, in July, 1774'. I should guess that the rector of Cranford was about twenty-seven years of age when he wrote those letters; and Miss Matty told me that her mother was just eighteen at the time of her wedding. With my idea of the rector, derived from a picture in the dining-parlour, stiff and stately, in a huge full-bottomed wig, with gown, cassock, and bands, and his hand upon a copy of the only sermon he ever published—it was strange to read these letters. They were full of eager, passionate ardour; short homely sentences, right fresh from the heart—(very different from the grand Latinised, Johnsonian style of the printed sermon, preached before some judge at assizes time). His letters were a curious contrast to those of his girl-bride. She was evidently rather annoyed at his demands upon her for expressions of love, and could not quite understand what he meant by repeating the same thing over in so many different ways; but what she was quite clear about was her longing for a white 'Paduasoy',—whatever that might be; and six or seven letters were principally occupied in asking her lover to use his influence with her parents (who evidently kept her in good order) to obtain this or that article of dress, more especially the white 'Paduasoy'.... But at length he seemed to find out that she would not be married till she had a 'trousseau' to her mind; and then he sent her a letter, which had evidently accompanied a whole box full of finery, and in which he requested that she might be dressed in everything her heart desired.... Shortly afterwards they were married,—I suppose, from the intermission in their correspondence.

There was a great gap before any of the rector's letters appeared.... The letters were written on the occasion of the publication of the same Sermon which was represented in the picture. The preaching before 'My Lord Judge,' and the 'publishing

48

by request,' was evidently the culminating point—the event of his
life. It had been necessary for him to go up to London to superintend
it through the press. . . . The worthy rector seemed to be strung up
by the occasion to a high literary pitch, for he could hardly write a
letter to his wife without cropping out into Latin. I remember the end
of one of his letters ran thus:— 'I shall ever hold the virtuous qualities
of my Molly in remembrance, *dum memor ipse mei, dum spiritus
regit artus*,' which, considering that the English of his correspondent
was sometimes at fault in grammar, and often in spelling, might be
taken as a proof of how much he 'idealised his Molly'.

ELIZABETH GASKELL (1810—1865)

28.   Mrs Elton goes parish visiting ahead of her husband.

'Yes, here I am, my good friend,' said Mrs Elton, 'and here I
have been so long, that anywhere else I should think it necessary to
apologise: but the truth is, that I am waiting for my lord and master.
He promised to join me here, and pay his respects to you.'

'What! are we to have the pleasure of a call from Mr Elton?—That
will be a favour indeed! for I know gentlemen do not like morning
visits, and Mr Elton's time is so engaged.'

'Upon my word it is, Miss Bates. He really is engaged from morning to night.—There is no end of people's coming to him, on some
pretence or other. The magistrates, and overseers, and churchwardens, are always wanting his opinion. They seem not able to do anything without him. "Upon my word, Mr Elton, I often say, rather you
than I. I do not know what would become of my crayons and my
instrument, if I had half so many applicants". Bad enough as it is, for I
absolutely neglect them both to an unpardonable degree. I believe I
have not played a bar this fortnight. However, he is coming, I assure
you: yes, indeed, on purpose to wait on you all. . . . He promised to
come on to me as soon as he could disengage himself from
Knightley; but he and Knightley are shut up together in deep
consultation. . . . I do believe,' she continued, 'this is the most
troublesome parish that ever was. We never heard of such things at
Maple Grove.'

'Your parish there was small,' said Jane.

'Upon my word, my dear, I do not know, for I never heard the subject talked of . . . .'

Mr Elton made his appearance. His lady greeted him with some of
her sparkling vivacity.

'Very pretty, sir, upon my word; to send me on here, to be an
encumbrance to my friends, so long before you vouchsafe to
come!—But you knew what a dutiful creature you had to deal with.
You knew I should not stir till my lord and master appeared . . . .'

Mr Elton was so hot and tired, that all this wit seemed thrown away.
His civilities to the other ladies must be paid; but his subsequent

object was to lament over himself for the heat he was suffering, and
the walk he had had for nothing.

JANE AUSTEN (1775—1817)

29.   For the rest of the afternoon, Dahlia and Cecil and the charwoman were hard at work, moving furniture, emptying packing cases and arranging books and china, and by the time dusk had
fallen there was a semblance of order in the house and a bright little
fire in the sitting-room and Mrs Bailey carried away the remains of
the pressed beef and Dahlia's good opinion. Not once had she
protested against the reverend gentleman's menial labours or
paused to expostulate with Dahlia for standing on the top of the
steps to hang the curtains.

'I like that woman,' Dahlia said. 'Does she go regularly to church?'

'No, but she sends her children to Sunday School.'

'Good idea!' Dahlia said heartily, then, lifting her eyebrows
ruefully, she glanced at Cecil. It was the wrong comment, but he was
careful not to notice it.

'She has to cook the Sunday dinner,' he explained.

'And so shall I have to. But,' she added quickly, 'it will be the kind of
cooking that doesn't need much attention. A stew's the thing. It's
quite happy if it's left alone. Isn't it a mercy we shan't have to be
careful not to give the servant trouble?'

'I wish we could afford to have one. I don't see how you'll manage
to keep the house clean.'

'I shan't. Not very. But it's going to look pretty when I've finished
with it and, once a week, Mrs Bailey can come and scrub.'

'But there'll be callers soon,' he said, 'lots of callers. What are you
going to do about them?'

'What would you like me to do?' Dahlia asked.

E.H. YOUNG (1880—1949)

30.   Mrs Crawley, the rector's wife was a smart little body, who
wrote this worthy divine's sermons. Being of a domestic turn,

51

and keeping the house a great deal with her daughters, she ruled absolutely within the Rectory, wisely giving her husband full liberty without. He was welcome to come and go, and dine abroad as many days as his fancy dictated, for Mrs Crawley was a saving woman and knew the price of port wine. Ever since Mrs Bute carried off the young rector of Queen's Crawley...she had been a prudent and thrifty wife to him.

WILLIAM MAKEPEACE THACKERAY (1811—1863)

31.   I stand up and say, 'My name is Susan. I am a vicar's wife and I am an alcoholic.' Then I tell my story. Or some of it anyway. 'Don't pull any punches,' says Clem, my counsellor. 'Nobody's going to be shocked, believe me love, we've all been there. . . .'

'So how did you come to AA?' they ask. 'My husband,' I say. 'The vicar. He persuaded me. . . .'

So now everything has changed. For the moment I am a new woman and Geoffrey is a new man. And he brings it up on the slightest pretext. 'My wife's an alcoholic, you know. Yes. It's a great challenge to me and to the parish as extended family.' From being a fly in the ointment I find myself transformed into a feather in his cap. Included it in his sermon on Prayers Answered when he reveals that he and the fan club have been having these jolly get togethers in which they'd all prayed over what he calls 'my problem'. It practically sent me racing back to the Tio Pepe even to think of it. The fans, of course, never dreaming that their prayers would be answered, are furious. They think it's brought us closer together. Geoffrey thinks that too. We were at some doleful diocesan jamboree last week and I am stuck there clutching my grapefuit juice as Geoffrey's telling the tale to some bearded cleric. Suddenly he seizes my hand. 'We met it with love,' he cries, as if love were some all-purpose antibiotic, which to Geoffrey it probably is.

And it goes on, the mileage in it endless. I said to Geoffrey that when I stood up at AA I sometimes told the story about the flower arranging. Result: he starts telling it all over the diocese. The first time was at a conference on The Supportive Parish. Gales of deep,

52

liberated, caring laughter. He's now given it a new twist and tells the story as if he's talking about a parishioner, than at the end he says, 'Friends I want to tell you something. (Deep hush.) That drunken flower-arranger was my wife.' Silence . . . then the applause, *terrific*.

I've caught the other young, upwardly mobile parsons sneaking looks at me now and again and you can see them thinking why weren't they smart enough to marry an alcoholic or better still a drug addict, problem wives whom they could do a nice redemption job on, right there on their own doorstep. Because there's no stopping Geoffrey now. He grips my hand in public, nay *brandishes* it. 'We're a team,' he cries. Looks certain to be rural dean and that's only the beginning. As the bishop says, 'Just the kind of man we're looking for on the bench . . . someone with a seasoned compassion, someone who's looked life in the face. Someone who's been there.'

ALAN BENNETT (1934—   )

32.   With the healthy shame of a child, Margaret blamed herself for her keenness of sight, in perceiving that all was not as it should be in Helstone parsonage. Her mother—her mother always so kind and tender towards her—seemed now and then so much discontented with this situation; thought that the bishop strangely neglected his episcopal duties, in not giving Mr Hale a better living; and almost reproached her husband because he could not bring himself to say that he wished to leave the parish, and undertake the charge of a larger. He would sigh aloud as he answered, that if he could do what he ought in little Helstone, he should be thankful; but everyday he was more overpowered; the world became more bewildering. At each repeated urgency of his wife, that he would put himself in the way of seeking some preferment, Margaret saw that her father shrank more and more; and she strove at such times to reconcile her mother to Helstone. Mrs Hale said that the near neighbourhood of so many trees affected her health. . . .

The evenings were rather difficult to fill up. Immediately after tea her father withdrew into his small library, and she and her mother were left alone. Mrs Hale had never cared much for books, and had

53

discouraged her husband, very early in their married life, in his desire of reading aloud to her, while she worked. At one time they had tried backgammon as a resource; but as Mr Hale grew to take an increasing interest in his school and his parishioners, he found that the interruptions which arose out of these duties were regarded as hardships by his wife, not to be accepted as the natural conditions of his profession, but to be regretted and struggled against by her as they severally arose. So he withdrew, while the children were yet young, into his library, to spend his evenings (if he were at home), in reading the speculative and metaphysical books which were his delight.

ELIZABETH GASKELL (1810—1865)

33.   The increased self-consciousness of women in the Church, together with increased concern about clergy wives, prompted me after nearly thirty years in orders and service in three provinces of the Anglican Communion to analyse the clergy wives that I have known. These are the findings.

First, what are the complaints? A clergy wife is regarded as dowdy cheap labour. She is thought of as part of the ministerial operation in a parish. She is expected to be associated with her husband in all his work in the clerical role, except those things which he alone can do. Thus the wife infers that she is expected: to take messages, to deputise for her husband when he is unavailable in such things as taking details of baptisms and weddings, to provide meals and light refreshments as may be required by her husband and/or the parish whether it be for diocesan, deanery or parochial people, to arrange flowers, or arrange for the flowers to be arranged, to organize and take a leading part in the cleaning of the church, the hall, and any other premises there may be, to organize at least some significant part of any fund raising efforts (probably refreshments) and to put in a major effort at the stall concerned, to assist, if need be, in the care of other people's children, on churchly occasions, to be the 'Queen Bee' in all female organizations, to shoulder her role in the PCC, but not to be argumentative in it, to call in upon parishioners who might desire it, particularly the sick, to listen to opinions of her husband, to wear a hat, to have time to chat, to provide materials, food and gossip to 'gentlemen of the road', to assist in the Sunday School if need be, to assist with the confirmation candidates, to go on the congregational outing and other social events, and that may not be all. She may be the confidante of her husband; and allow it to be assumed that she is.

JOHN ROGAN (1928—   )

Daughters

34.   It was the latter part of July when Margaret returned home to
        the country parsonage at Helstone where her parents lived.
The forest trees were all one dark, full, dusky green; the fern below
them caught all the slanting sunbeams; the weather was sultry and
broodingly still. Margaret used to tramp along by her father's side,
crushing down the fern with a cruel glee, as she felt it yield under her
light foot, and send up the fragrance peculiar to it,—out on the broad
commons into the warm scented light, seeing multitudes of wild,
free, living creatures, revelling in the sunshine, and the herbs and
flowers it called forth. This life—at least these walks—realised all
Margaret's anticipations. She took a pride in her forest. Its people
were her people. She made hearty friends with them; learned and
delighted in using their peculiar words; took up her freedom
amongst them; nursed their babies, talked or read with slow
distinctness to their old people; carried dainty messes to their sick;
resolved before long to teach at the school, where her father went
every day as to an appointed task, but she was continually tempted
off to go and see some individual friend—man, woman, or child—in
some cottage in the green shade of the forest. Her out-of-doors life
was perfect.

ELIZABETH GASKELL (1810—1865)

35.   Juliet and Imogen found their father talking to the Club Secre-
        tary. 'Hello,' he said, 'have some tea.' And went back to his
conversation.

A savage example of the Church Militant, the Reverend Stephen
Brocklehurst had one great secular passion—sport. He was now
giving the Club Secretary a blow by blow account of why Nicky
Beresford had played so badly.

'The boy was overconfident, of course; thought he had the whole
thing sewn up.'

Juliet giggled and applied herself to the cucumber sandwiches.

56

Imogen sat in a dream, until Juliet nudged her. 'Beresford's just walked in,' she hissed.

Imogen choked over her tea. Everyone was hailing him from all corners.

'He's seen you,' whispered Juliet. 'He's working his way in this direction.'

'Hello Nicky,' said the Club Secretary. 'Whatever happened to you?'

Beresford laughed, showing very white teeth. 'I saw something I fancied on the other side of the netting,' he said, looking at Imogen.

'You ought to play in blinkers,' said the Club Secretary. 'Come and join us. Have you met our vicar, Mr Brocklehurst, and his daughters, Imogen and Juliet?'

'No, I haven't,' said Beresford, shaking hands and holding Imogen's hand for longer than necessary before he sat down between her and the vicar.

'Brocklehurst,' he said reflectively, as he dropped four lumps of sugar into his tea. 'Brocklehurst? Weren't you capped for England just after the war?'

Mr Brocklehurst melted like butter in a heatwave.

'Yes indeed. Clever of you to remember that.'

After talking to the vicar about rugger for five minutes, and having wangled himself an invitation to lunch next day, Beresford turned his attention to Imogen.

'Well, you certainly threw me,' he said softly. 'It's a good thing there weren't any Davis Cup selectors about.'

'I'm so pleased you won,' stammered Imogen.

'And I'm pleased,' he looked straight into her eyes, 'that you're even more beautiful close up.'

So was he, thought Imogen. Far more beautiful, with dark smudges under his eyes, and damp tendrils curling round his forehead. His voice was low and confiding as though she were the only person in the world he wanted to talk to.

And although he asked the usual questions—What did she do for a living? Did she enjoy it? Did she ever come to London?—his smoky voice, and the way his eyes wandered over her body and her face, made even those familiar phrases sound significant. . . .

'Where d'you play next?' she asked. The thought of him going away was already unbearable.

Nicky grinned. 'Rome on Monday, Paris the week after, then Edinburgh, Wimbledon, Gstaad, Kitzbuhel, and then the North American circuit, Washington, Indianapolis, Toronto, finally Forest Hills, if I don't die of exhaustion.'

Imogen gasped. Scotland was the most abroad she'd ever been to.

'Oh, how lovely,' she said. 'Think of the postcards one could send.'

Nicky laughed. 'I could face it if you came with me,' he said, lowering his voice.

Imogen blushed and gazed into her tea cup. . . .

The loudspeaker hiccupped and announced the finals of the men's doubles. Reluctantly Nicky got to his feet.

'There's a party here this evening, I wondered if you—and your sister, of course,' he added smiling at Juliet, 'would like to come?'

'Oh, yes please,' began Imogen, but the vicar promptly looked round.

'Good of you to ask them,' he said blandly, 'but I'm afraid they've already been booked to help at the Mothers' Union whist drive. We shall look forward to seeing you at lunch tomorrow, any time after half past twelve.'

Both Imogen and Juliet opened their mouths in protest, then shut them again. They knew their father. Just for a second Nicky's eyes narrowed. Then he smiled.

'I shall look forward to it too,' he said. . . .

'Don't you sometimes wish Daddy had been an engineer?' said Juliet, as she and Imogen trailed home.

JILLY COOPER (1937—   )

36. Mr Allaby was rector of Campsford, a village a few miles from Cambridge. He, too, had taken a good degree, had got a fellowship, and in the course of time had accepted a college living of about £400 a year and a house. His private income did not exceed £200 a year. On resigning his fellowship he married a woman a good

deal younger than himself who bore him eleven children, nine of whom—two sons and seven daughters—were living. The two eldest daughters had married fairly well, but at the time of which I am now writing there were still five unmarried. . . .

Mrs Allaby talked about having married two of her daughters as though it had been the easiest thing in the world. She talked in this way because she heard other mothers do so, but in her heart of hearts she did not know how she had done it, nor indeed if it had been her doing at all. First there had been a young man in connection with whom she had tried to practise certain manoeuvres which she had rehearsed in imagination over and over again, but which she found impossible to apply in practice. Then there had been weeks of *wurra wurra* of hopes and fears and little strategems which as often as not proved injudicious, and then somehow or other in the end, there lay the young man bound and with an arrow through his heart at her daughter's feet. It seemed to her to be all a fluke which she could have little or no hope of repeating. She had indeed repeated it once, and might perhaps with good luck repeat it yet once again—but five times over! It was awful: why, she would rather have three confinements than go through the wear and tear of marrying a single daughter.

Nevertheless it had got to be done, and poor Mrs Allaby never looked at a young man without an eye to his being a future son-in-law. Papas and mammas sometimes ask young men whether their intentions are honourable towards their daughters. I think young men might occasionally ask papas and mammas whether their intentions are honourable before they accept invitations to houses where there are still unmarried daughters.

SAMUEL BUTLER (1835—1902)

37.   Deborah said to me, the day of my mother's funeral, that if she had a hundred offers, she never would marry and leave my father. It was not very likely she would have so many—I don't know that she had one; but it was not less to her credit to say so. She was such a daughter to my father, as I think there never was before, or

59

since. His eyes failed him, and she read book after book, and wrote, and copied, and was always at his service in any parish business. She could do many more things than my poor mother could; she even once wrote a letter to the bishop for my father. But he missed my mother sorely; the whole parish noticed it. Not that he was less active; I think he was more so, and more patient in helping everyone. I did all I could to set Deborah at liberty to be with him; for I knew I was good for little, and that my best work in the world was to do odd jobs quietly, and set others at liberty.

ELIZABETH GASKELL (1810—1865)

38.   Mrs Bates, the widow of a former vicar of Highbury, was a very old lady, almost past everything but tea and quadrille. She lived with her single daughter in a very small way, and was considered with all the regard and respect which a harmless old lady, under such untoward circumstances, can excite. Her daughter enjoyed a most uncommon degree of popularity for a woman neither young, handsome, rich, nor married. Miss Bates stood in the very worst predicament in the world for having much of the public favour; and she had no intellectual superiority to make atonement to herself, or frighten those who might hate her, into outward respect. She had never boasted either beauty or cleverness. Her youth had passed without distinction, and her middle of life was devoted to the care of a failing mother, and the endeavour to make a small income go as far as possible. And yet she was a happy woman, and a woman whom no one named without good-will. It was her own universal good-will and contented temper which worked such wonders. She loved everybody, and was interested in everybody's happiness, quick-sighted to everybody's merits; thought herself a most fortunate creature, and surrounded with blessings in such an excellent mother and so many good neighbours and friends, and a home that wanted for nothing. The simplicity and cheerfulness of her nature, her contented and grateful spirit, were a recommendation to everybody and a mine of felicity to herself. She was a great talker upon little matters, which exactly suited Mr

60

Woodhouse, full of trivial communications and harmless gossip. . . .

The house belonged to people in business. Mrs and Miss Bates occupied the drawing-room floor; and there, in the very moderate sized apartment, which was everything to them, the visitors were most cordially and even gratefully welcomed; the quiet neat old lady, who with her knitting was seated in the warmest corner, wanting even to give up her place to Miss Woodhouse, and her more active, talking daughter, almost ready to overpower them with care and kindness, thanks for their visit, solicitude for their shoes, anxious inquiries after Mr Woodhouse's health, cheerful communications about her mother's, and sweet-cake from the beaufet.

JANE AUSTEN (1775—1817)

62

Parsonages

39.   It was settled that the whole party should drive over on the following day to inspect the parsonage at St Ewold. The three
clergymen were to discuss dilapidations, and the two ladies were to
lend their assistance in suggesting such changes as might be
necessary for a bachelor's abode. Accordingly, soon after breakfast,
the carriage was at the door. . . .

Archdeacon Grantly was soon making speeches about wounded
roofs and walls, which he declared to be in want of some surgeon's
art. There was not a partition that he did not tap, nor a block of
chimneys that he did not narrowly examine; all water-pipes, flues,
cisterns, and sewers underwent an investigation; and he even
descended, in the care of his friend, so far as to bore sundry boards in
the floors with a bradawl.

Mr Arabin accompanied him through the rooms, trying to look
wise in such domestic matters, and the other three also followed. Mrs
Grantly showed that she had not herself been priestess of a parish
twenty years for nothing, and examined the bells and window panes
in a very knowing way. . . .

Here they were interrupted by the archdeacon, whose voice was
heard from the cellar shouting to the vicar.

'Arabin, Arabin,'—and then turning to his wife, who was
apparently at his elbow—'where has he gone to? This cellar is
perfectly abominable. It would be murder to put a bottle of wine into
it till it has been roofed, walled, and floored. How on earth old
Goodenough ever got on with it, I cannot guess. But then
Goodenough never had a glass of wine that any man could drink.'

'What is it, archdeacon?' said the vicar, running down stairs. . . .

'This cellar must be roofed, walled, and floored,' repeated the
archdeacon. 'Now mind what I say, and don't let the architect persuade you that it will do; half of these fellows know nothing about
wine. This place as it is now would be damp and cold in winter, and
hot and muggy in summer. I wouldn't give a straw for the best wine
that ever was vinted, after it had lain here a couple of years.'

Mr Arabin assented, and promised that the cellar should be reconstructed according to the archdeacon's receipt.

'And, Arabin, look here; was such an attempt at a kitchen grate ever seen?'

'The grate is really very bad,' said Mrs Grantly. . . .

By this time the archdeacon had again ascended, and was now in the dining-room. 'Arabin,' said he, speaking in his usual loud clear voice, and with that tone of dictation which was so common to him; 'you must positively alter this dining-room, that is remodel it altogether; look here, it is just sixteen feet by fifteen; did anybody ever hear of a dining-room of such proportions!' and the archdeacon stepped the room long-ways and cross-ways with ponderous steps, as though a certain amount of ecclesiastical dignity could be imparted even to such an occupation as that by the manner of doing it. 'Barely sixteen; you may call it a square.'

Mr Arabin, however, did not appear well inclined to enter into speculative expenses, and therefore, any material alterations in the house, the cost of which could not fairly be made to lie at the door either of the ecclesiastical commissioners or of the estate of the late incumbent, were tabooed. With this essential exception, the archdeacon ordered, suggested, and carried all points before him in a manner very much to his own satisfaction.

ANTHONY TROLLOPE (1815—1882)

40.   It is equally impossible for the rector to shepherd his flock (as he does, conscientiously) and, single-handed, keep nearly three acres of garden in order, to say nothing of maintaining the house and the crumbling outbuildings in repair. . . .

Mr Follows has often thought of shutting up most of the Rectory; but he realises, as his critics do not, that an empty house deteriorates. The dry-rotting roof, for which he knows he is responsible, is enough to be going on with; he will not take on any more risks. Nor is he, it must be granted, unduly querulous, though one might fancy that it is the weight of this Rectory that gives his shoulders their slight stoop and furrows his high and rather narrow forehead under the biretta he wears to keep the draught off his natural tonsure when he turns his back on his troubles and crosses the road to the church.

Even when he thinks most hardly of the Rectory he cannot help remembering the thrill he experienced when first he set eyes on it, at Miss Abberley's invitation, sixteen years ago. If it were not for the virginia creeper that smothers it and the overgrown laurels and conifers that hide its facade and which, if he could afford the time and the money to pay for felling and uprooting them, Mr Follows would certainly destroy, the sight of the Rectory would add to the dignity of the Cross. It was built, to the taste of an ecclesiastical Abberley, of the same material as The Grange, but a little later, and is a pure example of the Queen Anne style: a square, solid three-storeyed building with rows of well-proportioned windows and bricked-up apertures where, but for the tax, other windows would have been. Since Mr Follows came to live there it has never been adequately furnished, for he was too poor to buy the curtains that went for a song at his predecessor's sale, and the filling of such an enormous window-space with new ones was beyond his most extravagant dreams. As a makeshift, which has become permanent, Mrs Follows ingeniously fitted the windows in the rooms they try to occupy with lengths of casement-cloth which, though they exclude little light, give these handsome chambers an odd air of nakedness.

FRANCIS BRETT YOUNG (1884—1954)

41.   Into the silence fell at long intervals the croaking caw of a rook,
       intensifying the quiet. In the garden the rambler roses blazed, the lilies stood each in an aura of stillness that was about the flowers like light round the moon. Nothing stirred except the Rector's bees, who seemed to think of taking an unfair advantage of his siesta by swarming. The Rector, in his cool, green-lit drawing-room, was having his usual conscientious Sabbath slumber over Paley's 'Evidences'. The good man always did violence to his wishes on Sunday, putting away all his books on gems, not so much as cutting the leaves of the latest brochure on diamonds, though it had only arrived on Saturday. Paley was dutifully opened after dinner, but the house was so quiet (Rectory-Lucy being out and even the cat sleeping the

sleep of repletion) that a bland complacency came over his thoughts. He pondered on his good fortune in having avoided matrimony, and a great peace overwhelmed him, so that Paley remained where Paley had been opened at half-past two. This weakness of the Rector's was bitter to Ernest, who was unable to see what a much better parish priest the Rector made simply because he could not read Paley. When the Rector sat in his armchair and slept rosily, the veriest sinner must have confided in him; and while his intellectual light gave an uncertain ray, his humanity shone like a lighthouse upon all who came near him.

MARY WEBB (1881—1927)

42.   Before twelve o'clock there had been some heavy storms of rain, and the water lay in deep gutters on the side of the gravel-walks in the garden of Broxton Parsonage; the great Provence roses had been cruelly tossed by the wind and beaten by the rain, and all the delicate-stemmed border flowers had been dashed down and stained with the wet soil. A meloncholy morning. . . .

But people who have pleasant homes get indoor enjoyments that they would never think of but for the rain. If it had not been a wet morning, Mr Irwine would not have been in the dining-room playing at chess with his mother, and he loves both his mother and chess quite well enough to pass some cloudy hours very easily by their help. Let me take you into that dining-room, and show you the Rev. Adolphus Irwine, Rector of Broxton, Vicar of Hayslope, and Vicar of Blythe, a pluralist at whom the severest Church reformer would have found it difficult to look sour. We will enter very softly, and stand still in the green doorway, without awaking the glossy-brown setter who is stretched across the hearth, with her two puppies beside her; or the pug, who is dozing, with his black muzzle aloft, like a sleepy president.

The room is a large and lofty one, with an ample mullioned oriel window at one end; the walls, you see, are new, and not yet painted; but the furniture, though originally of an expensive sort, is old and scanty, and there is no drapery about the window. The crimson cloth over the large dining-table is very threadbare, though it contrasts pleasantly enough with the dead hue of the plaster on the walls; but on this cloth there is a massive silver waiter with a decanter of water on it, of the same pattern as two larger ones that are propped up on the sideboard with a coat of arms conspicuous in their centre. You suspect at once that the inhabitants of the room have inherited more blood than wealth. . . .

'There, Dauphin, tell me what that is!' says the magnificent old lady, as she deposits her queen very quietly and folds her arms. 'I should be sorry to utter a word disagreeable to your feelings.'

'Ah! you witch-mother, you sorceress! How is a Christian man to win a game off you? I should have sprinkled the board with holy water before we began. You've not won that game by fair means, now, so don't pretend it.'

'Yes, yes, that's what the beaten have always said of great con-querors. But, see, there's the sunshine falling on the board, to show you more clearly what a foolish move you made with that pawn. Come, shall I give you another chance?'

'No, mother, I shall leave you to your own conscience, now its clearing up. We must go and plash up the mud a little, mustn't we, Juno?' This was addressed to the brown setter, who had jumped up at the sound of the voices and laid her nose in an insinuating way on her master's leg.

GEORGE ELIOT (1819—1880)

43.   The vicarage turned out to be in a small wood. Of course it hadn't been built in one: the saplings planted by some earlier incumbent as garden features had become immense spreading trees, and their undergrowth had blotted out any lawns or flower beds that may once have been there. In fact, the drive was now a tunnel and the scuffle of my boots sent wood-pigeons threshing through branches and boughs into the sky. And, round a turn, I came across a hare: it gazed in amazement at me. A jay flew across. A jay! I'd only seen one in books. Why the place was a latter-day Eden!

The house was in a clearing, but what once had been a drive-around for carriages was now blocked by a vast stricken cedar, its torn roots heaving up like a cliff-side and supporting a town-sized garden, its crevices already colonised by wild plants. The once white bricks of the house walls had taken on a unpleasing greenish tinge so that they had a damp look, the windows were mostly shuttered and the building's squarish severity was only ameliorated by a twin-pillared portico. . . . . I knocked at the door and then dragged the bell. . . .

My several well-mannered tugs were unanswered and, had I not been penniless, I would have gone away. So, quite annoyed by this time, I gave the thing a really savage drag. A good six inches of wire scraped from the hole and, when released, shot back like a catapult. Deep inside the house I heard a bell tinkling, like distant laughter. As a matter of fact, for a moment, I believed it was someone laughing at me. . . .

Feeling vaguely guilty, I looked around. Really it was quite oppressive and I marvelled that any practising novel-reader dared put a nose beyond the door at night: an entire tribe of thugs come to retrieve green eyes from little yellow gods stolen by an incumbent's ne'er-do-well brother could have camped there unseen for weeks. As for the vicarage, it could have housed a family of ten with supporting coachmen, cooks, maids and all. Where it was plain that the Revd J.G. Keach could not afford a gardener.

Then the white-painted door opened and Alice Keach looked

out. . . . She was overwrought and, before I had time to ask if I might see her husband, she had come out upon the portico and had launched into a rather wild account of what it was like living there, as though she mistook me for a diocesan investigator of clerical dwellings. . . .

It was astonishing. Here I was, almost a stranger, being told of a most alarming nightmare she'd been having—how trees had been closing in on her, first swaying menacingly, then dragging up their roots and actually advancing, closing in until mercifully fended off at the last minute by the house walls.

J.L. CARR (1912—   )

44.   The Rectory was a delightful Regency building, almost hidden behind walls which would have done justice to a prison.

Once inside the gates, the front garden was a joy to behold. There was nothing formal about it. It was really a back-to-nature effort, and consisted mainly of vast numbers of uninhibited hollyhocks interspersed with hordes of unchecked dandelions which were much bigger and more flamboyant than any I had ever dug out of the lawn at home.

The lawn in this case was unique and full of character, wandering all over the paths and half way up the front steps. And gracing the whole scene, adding that indefinable old-world touch, there stood in the centre of the lawn a twenty-ton traction engine.

The rector, opening the door and noting the admiration on my face, explained eagerly that he was the chairman of the local traction engine society which held those breath-taking, exciting races over ploughed fields every bank holiday.

I said I was grateful that at least *some* people were saving the steam-engine from extinction, and, beaming, he led me into a large kitchen-like apartment with a stone-flagged floor.

As it was a rather chilly evening, he drew up a settle in front of a magnificent black and brass range which stretched along one entire wall.

The rector, a middle-aged unobtrusive type, was apparently a

69

bachelor, and pointed out that notwithstanding its beauties the house was perhaps just a little inconvenient for him, having twelve bedrooms, no bathrooms, no domestic staff, and the aforementioned range which burned about half a ton of coal a day and provided stone-cold water in every part of the house at all times.

No one lived with him, but in the cathedral-like stables at the rear of the rectory he nurtured a gigantic Shire horse who kept winning prizes at agricultural shows—and never did any work at all. He did, however, obviate the necessity of mowing the lawn.

REGINAL FRARY (1920—   )

45.   The Rev. Frank Fenwick passed up through the garden, and, when he was near the terrace which ran along the garden front of the house, he thought that he heard a voice. He stood under the shade of a wall dark with ivy, and distinctly heard whispering on the other side of it. As far as he could tell there were the voices of more than two men. . . . Standing where he was he would probably be able to interrupt them, should they attempt to enter the house; but in the mean time they might be stripping his fruit from the wall. They were certainly, at present, in the kitchen garden, and he was not minded to leave them there at such work as they might have in hand. Having paused to think of this, he crept along under the wall, close to the house, towards the passage by which he could reach them. But they had not heard him, nor had they waited among the fruit. When he was near the corner of the wall, one leading man came round within a foot or two of the spot on which he stood; and, before he could decide on what he would do, the second had appeared. He rushed forward with the loaded stick in his hand, but, knowing its weight, and remembering the possibility of the comparative innocence of the intruders, he hesitated to strike. A blow on the head would have brained a man, and a knock on the arm with such an instrument would break the bone. In a moment he found his left hand on the leading man's throat, and the man's foot behind his heel. He fell, but as he fell he did strike heavily, cutting upwards with his weapon, and bringing the heavy weight of lead at the end of it on

to the man's shoulder. He stumbled rather than fell, but when he regained his footing, the man was gone. That man was gone, and the others were following him down towards the gate at the bottom of the orchard. Of these two, in a few strides, he was able to catch the hindermost, and then he found himself wrestling with Sam Brattle.

'Sam,' said he, speaking as well as he could with his short breath, 'if you don't stand, I'll strike you with the life-preserver.'

Sam made another struggle, trying to seize the weapon, and the parson hit him with it on the right arm.

'You've smashed that anyway, Mr Fenwick,' said the man.

'I hope not; but do you come along with me quietly, or I'll smash something else. I'll hit you on the head if you attempt to move away. What were you doing here?'

ANTHONY TROLLOPE (1815—1882)

HAYMAKING

Staff

46.   By modern standards the house was badly lit. . . . The front
hall had a table lamp near the bottom of the stairs in the inner
hall. There was a hanging, counterpoise lamp in the outer hall, but
seldom used. The long passage had one wall lamp as did the upstairs
passage, placed outside the nursery door. The kitchen had a
hanging lamp as also the servants hall. . . . All bedrooms were lit by
candle, two on the dressing table; the last job of the housemaid was
to light these in the principal bedrooms. On going to bed one took
one of the many silver candlesticks from the hall table, lighted it and
took it to the room. This was the bedside light. A box of matches was
kept by it. It was the duty of the housemaid to trim the lamps every
day. This was done in the pantry. A large drum of paraffin, about fifty
gallons, was kept in the 'oil place' in the stable yard and one gallon
cans filled from it. Trimming meant filling, trimming the wick,
cleaning the chimney and if brass, keeping the whole polished. . . .

A large amount of coal was burned in the rectory fires of which
there were a great many. The kitchen range alone must have used
between one or two hundred-weight a day according to the cooking.
All the open fires were very uneconomical and badly designed. In
spite of stocking up, carts made frequent journeys to Donisthorpe
pit. . . .

The rectory was large and required a large staff inside and as we
farmed the glebe there was also an outside staff. Of the rectory
indoor staff I can just remember the butler, William Savage. For
some reason I was reprimanded for calling him Bill. I was very upset
at this, went to Bill and said 'I'm not to call you Bill any more but I can
still call you Mungo'. That was the name I had called him since I was
able to make a noise like talking. We were never allowed to call the
men by their Christian names, always by their surnames, except the
garden boy. Savage went soon after this to be caretaker of Kirkstead
House, an estate in Lincolnshire which my father owned. We never
had another butler. The first parlourmaid I remember was Emma
Mee. She was followed by Lucy Smith, a local girl, and then by a series of others, Annie Harden from Burton, Annie Sizer from

Gainsborough, both called Emma so as not to be confused with Annie Reeves, and finally Lilly Butcher, from Woodhall, the best and most proficient of all. Annie Reeves was cook, a very good one. There were various junior maids coming and going. Upstairs, Nell Guy reigned, assisted by nursery maids who came and went which was not to be wondered at. I can hardly remember any except Hetty from Norton who suffered severely from our antics.

The first groom I remember was Charles Aucott who came from and returned to Repton. He was followed by Harry Farmer who came to us from Cliff House, Twycross, where the Oakleys lived. Farmer left us to go to the Hall as second horseman to Smith, the stud groom. Their man, Thomas Gregory, came to us after a short break and stayed with us until the end of the war. He married a girl from Ashby and in due course they produced a son. He was christened Vernon and at the gathering afterwards mother remarked how good the baby had been. The reply was 'just eight spots of whisky mum'. Not many people go drunk to their own christening!

Gregory was a good groom and a good horseman. He turned his horses out beautifully, whether for riding or carriage. They had to be good to satisfy father. After hunting—and we were sometimes quite late—the horses had to be groomed, fed and bedded down, the tackle cleaned and put away, not a thing to be left to the next day....

Charlie Bowley was gardener but, with a boy to help him, he also did other chores including cleaning boots, knives (they were all steel blades), filling the copper with soft water for the baths and lighting the fire early. Filling the many coal boxes, heating the oven on baking days and generally keeping the place clean.

One of the twice daily jobs was to pump water from the hard water pump to the supply tank for the kitchen hot water system and to the tank high in the roof above the pantry which fed the flush of the upstairs and only loo.

This pump, close to the scullery window, was a force pump. A screw cap was fitted on the spout, the rod worked in a gland and so held the pressure to force the water. It was easy pumping to the kitchen, but upstairs which Bowley called 'Klondyke', was hard going. This tank also filled by rain water. Many a night Bowley would look at the sky and declare it was going to rain so did not pump upstairs.

The men were paid on Saturday night after work. They gathered in the scullery and went in turn to the kitchen to be given their sovereign and discuss things. Harvest gave them a bit extra. For a year or two each was given a cask of beer for harvest. Winter and Bowley took theirs home but Gregory kept his in the apple house and it did not last long.

As would be expected, the rectory had a large garden and orchard. With the lawns there was a full-time job for a man and boy, as well as the chores.

AUBREY MOORE (1893—   )

47.   The vicar, an elderly bachelor, had depended on Mrs Jones for years to clean and cook, wash and iron, and cosset him with hot soup and mustard baths when he caught a chill. She even kept his geraniums watered in the conservatory. Now, of a sudden, this paragon of all the virtues had been struck down.... Little Miss Lovell—a tiny scrap of a woman, with a reputation for being excessively houseproud—was first on the doorstep to offer her services to the poor man. In less than ten minutes, she had donned an apron and was vigorously polishing the brass door knocker. From that moment, the Reverend Roger Coxall, six feet tall in his stockinged feet, was completely in the hands of the indefatigable little Martha. She attacked the cleaning of the big, old-fashioned house with such enthusiasm, the poor man was obliged to remove his boots in the hall and put on slippers. The floors were so slippery with polish he trod with great caution, fearful of falling and breaking a limb. The only room in the house where he was determined to be unmolested was the small study at the back of the house, overlooking a rather neglected garden. This was his private sanctum, and when he found his new housekeeper tidying the notes of his Sunday sermon, he was prompted to say, quite severely,

75

'Thank you, Martha, but I prefer not to have my desk disturbed, and neither does it require polishing.'

Martha was surprised and a little indignant, but packed up the hoover, the tin of polish and the dusters, and went out of the room, closing the door with a slam. The vicar sighed and thoughtfully scratched his chin.

'Such a splendid little woman; a pity to upset her, but sometimes one must insist on one's rights,' he murmured.

SARAH SHEARS

48.   I must now turn to another relation, concerning our own family: Joe and Sarah are going to be married, though I cannot exactly say when. They have mentioned their intentions sometime ago, but at the same time could not tell how to bring themselves to part with us. They are very desirous of still keeping their places, if we give them leave; and indeed they are both such good servants, and have such a regard for the interest of us and our family, that we cannot help being willing to comply with their requests; for they are now entering upon their fifteenth year, and I am pretty sure we shall never get two such in their places, who are so well acquainted with all our ways, and whom we could put such confidence in, for I verily believe there cannot be two people of more upright principles in all respects: and indeed just at this time, it would be very inconvenient to part with them, for our cook maid leaves us the 1st of next month; not that we have any objection at all to her, for she is a very cleanly, good servant but I find she has a prospect of advancing herself; therefore we would not be her hindrance: so we have concluded, that they shall stay with us; and if we find that any inconveniences are likely to arise from their having children, we have agreed to part; though I fancy (as she is between forty and fifty) there may be none at all: when the wedding is to be, I know not, for they intend to be asked in the church, and I have had no notice of it yet.

GEORGE WOODWARD (1708—1790)

76

49.   The vicar just left a widower was at this time a man about forty years of age, of good family, and childless. He had led a secluded existence in this college living, partly because there were no resident landowners; and his loss now intensified his habit of withdrawal from outward observation. He was seen still less than heretofore, kept himself still less in time with the rhythm and racket of the movements called progress in the world without. For many months after his wife's decease the economy of his household remained as before; the cook, the housemaid, the parlour-maid, and the man out-of-doors performed their duties or left them undone, just as Nature prompted them—the vicar knew not which. It was then represented to him that his servants seemed to have nothing to do in his small family of one. He was struck with the truth of this representation, and decided to cut down his establishment. But he was forestalled by Sophy, the parlour-maid, who said one evening that she wished to leave him.

'And why?' said the parson.

'Sam Hobson has asked me to marry him, sir.'

'Well—do you want to marry?'

'Not much. But it would be a home for me. And we have heard that one of us will have to leave.'

A day or two after she said: 'I don't want to leave just yet, sir, if you don't wish it. Sam and I have quarrelled.'

He looked up at her. He had hardly ever observed her before, though he had been frequently conscious of her soft presence in the room. What a kitten-like, flexuous, tender creature she was! She was the only one of the servants with whom he came into immediate and continuous relation. What should he do if Sophy were gone?'

Sophy did not go, but one of the others did, and things went on quietly again.

When Mr Twycott, the vicar, was ill, Sophy brought up his meals to him, and she had no sooner left the room one day than he heard a noise on the stairs. She had slipped down with the tray, and so twisted her foot that she could not stand. The village surgeon was called in; the vicar got better, but Sophy was incapacitated for a long time; and she was informed that she must never again walk much or engage in any occupation which required her to stand long on her feet. As soon as she was comparatively well she spoke to him alone. Since she was forbidden to walk and bustle about, and, indeed, could not do so, it became her duty to leave. She could very well work at something sitting down, and she had an aunt a seamstress.

The parson had been very greatly moved by what she had suffered on his account, and he exclaimed, 'No, Sophy; lame or not lame, I cannot let you go. You must never leave me again!'

He came close to her, and, though she could never exactly tell how it happened, she became conscious of his lips upon her cheek. He then asked her to marry him. Sophy did not exactly love him, but she had a respect for him which almost amounted to veneration. Even if she had wished to get away from him she hardly dared refuse a personage so reverend and august in her eyes, and she assented forthwith to be his wife.

THOMAS HARDY (1840—1928)

Pets

50.   The bell pull responded jerkily and, after an interval during
      which I imagined wires and rusty wheels wearily transmitting
my call, a bell rang faintly within the depths of the house. I waited,
clutching my case in a silence broken only by the heavy drips falling
irregularly from the sodden leaves. I was on the point of giving the
round black knob a second tug, when I was aware of a shuffling
sound and, with the drawing of the bolt, the door juddered open.

White hair was the only distinguishing feature, the rest of the frail
figure in shabby clerical black and faded collar being hard to
distinguish against the drab background, but there was no doubt it
was the Reverend Gladstone.

'You've come to see Tess,' he said, quietly. A gentle but sad smile
played upon his drawn features and he shivered slightly. 'Come
along in,' he beckoned. 'She's in the study.'

I followed the aged cleric across the gloomy hallway. Dark oil
paintings in heavy gilt frames hung from the walls and, as I passed a
stand laden with an untidy mix of coats and a collection of walking
sticks, I noticed some lady's hats hanging at the side. The Reverend
Gladstone, sensing my observation, said without turning: 'My dear
wife passed away last year, after much suffering. Sadly missed,' he
added, shaking his head. 'Sadly missed.' . . .

The Reverend Gladstone shuffled his carpet-slippered feet
towards the desk and leaned heavily upon it. He appeared to have
difficulty in getting his breath and, when he did, he gave a slight
cough and then pointed to the floor behind him. There, lying
prostrate before a one-bar electric fire, greying muzzle resting upon
a green pillow, her body partly covered by a patchwork blanket, was
an aged Red Setter.

'Tess,' said the old man affectionately. 'My Tess.'

Putting my case on the floor, I knelt beside the old dog and gently
drew back the blanket. Though her coat still shone, she was painfully
thin and her flanks slack and hollow. Laying my hand upon her chest
I felt her heart thumping irregularly and her breathing, though not
distressed, was very shallow.

'She started to falter two days ago,' he began. 'Until then she was eating quite well. Smaller meals than she used to, of course, and she took things a lot slower. Like we all must do,' he sighed. 'For some time she's been drinking more water than usual and I got some tablets for her kidneys. But she is fifteen and I became resigned that nothing could be done.'

Tess lay perfectly still and relaxed, quite oblivious to the discussion, but to me, it was obvious that her resistance was failing fast.

'I'm afraid that, for Tess, things are wearing out. Nothing lasts for ever,' I said.

'How right you are, young man,' replied the Reverend Gladstone. 'How right you are.' He moved unsteadily over to the armchair and, supporting himself upon its side, sat down. 'Fifteen years,' he continued, and his face took on another smile, but this time there was a more obvious thread of happiness in it, as memories of Tess and her companionship came flooding back.

He told me how, with his wife, he had returned from missionary work abroad to take the living at Brentdor.

'We bought her as a pup, when we moved in. She was so full of fun, my wife would play with her for hours on the lawn.' He raised his cloudy eyes towards the window. 'As I prepared my sermons, I could hear her laughter and Tess merrily barking in the garden.' . . .

I looked at the pathetic, crumpled old vicar in the armchair and knew I was getting involved. But after all, I reasoned, it was an old dog and what I was about to do was both practical and humane. Then I looked up at the old man again, the old man whose last link with his dear, departed wife and those happy, carefree days I was about to sever, and I realised there was far more to being a country vet than I had ever imagined.

He pressed his hands onto the arms of the chair, as if he was going to rise, but didn't.

'When my wife suffered so much pain in those last few weeks,' he said softly, 'there were times when I questioned my faith and wondered why it was all so necessary. At least, with Tess, I can repay her loyalty by not letting her linger.'

'Would you like to stay?' I asked.

He shook his head, then moved from the chair to kneel beside me. Shakily he bent forward and cradled the old Setter's head in his arms.

'Remember blackberry time, those warm, easeful days. We'd look for Molly in the fields; you'd see her first, old girl. She'd call and off you'd go, leaping across the stubble to her. Then I would catch you up and take her basket; then home we'd come, all three of us together.' He closed his eyes and pulled the old dog to him. 'Run on now, my Tess, to dear Molly. And I'll be with you shortly.'

He grabbed my arm as he rose and for a few seconds, head bowed, hung on to me. Then looking up, eyes tearful but still set with a gentle smile, he said:

'I'll leave her in your care, young man.' Then he shuffled to the door and drew it and the sagging curtain closed behind him.

I stood for a few seconds looking at her; I was full up and my eyes were feeling gritty, so I took a deep breath and opened the case.

Tess looked up momentarily as the fine needle entered her vein; then, as the barbiturate flooded her bloodstream, her breathing quickened slightly, she took two deeper breaths and lowered her head back onto her paws, as if she was very tired. Then she was still. Tess was dead, and I had killed her.

I pulled the patchwork blanket across and put the syringe and bottle away. After a few minutes I called the Reverend Gladstone; he offered me a sherry, but his hand shook so much that most of it spilled upon the floor. I asked if he would like me to take Tess away, but he declined, saying he would bury her in the garden. Then he walked with me to the gate and, as we parted, even asked God to bless me.

HUGH LASGARN (1933–   )

Hospitality

51. From outside, it was an ungracious house, a big rectangular
     box of granite that had been put up, I guessed, in mid-Victorian
times. Inside, it was cold, of a coldness that seemed to strike at you
palpably as you entered. We walked straight in through the open
door. I was to discover that Mr Savage never locked his door.
Sometimes he would remember to bang it shut before going to bed,
but as often as not it would remain open all night. During my stay
with him I once rose early and came down the stairs to be arrested,
fascinated, half-way by sight of a badger grunting and shuffling
about in the hall, sticking its snout into the row of dirty boots that
were always ranged there along the wall.

The hall, which was the first thing I saw of the vicarage, was paved
with stone, and so was every room on the ground floor. The hall was
more cloakroom than anything else. . . . The hats, old and rusty,
were on nails driven into the wall; the boots, that were never cleaned,
were ranged along the skirting-board, and the sticks which stood
wherever there was a corner to lean them into. . . . Amid this
paraphernalia in the hall a surplice fluttered. . . .

The house was dark as well as cold, for all the walls were painted in
a green that was almost black. And then my spirits rose quickly, for
on the landing Mr Savage opened a door and stood aside for me to
enter, and I walked into an airy lightness. . . .

I thanked him, and he said: 'The room opposite is my study. Come
across when you are ready. Then I'll make some tea'. . . .

There was no fire in the study, and it was getting colder. He had
boiled the kettle, a flimsy tin affair, on a Primus stove that stood in the
fireplace. The nauseating smell of methylated spirit filled the room,
and Mr Savage got up and opened the window. The sound of the
sea's surge came in. The tide was rising.

'I apologise,' he said, passing a plate of biscuits. 'I should have
liked to do something better for you.'

We drank the tea and ate the biscuits. . . . 'I think, you know,' Mr
Savage said, as though a really glorious idea had suddenly struck
him, 'we'd better have a fire.'

It seemed to me that for a man of his years he had had a heavy day. How far he had walked before I met him I did not know, but since then he had been in incessant movement. Not that he looked tired: far from it. But I said: 'If you will tell me where to find things, I'll see to the fire. And while I'm at it, I'll wash the cups.'

'Oh, it won't be so easy as that,' he said airily. 'It's more than a matter of finding things. There's wood to be cut. Come along.'

HOWARD SPRING (1889—1965)

52.   There, where a few torn shrubs the place disclose,
The village preacher's modest mansion rose.
A man he was to all the country dear,
And passing rich with forty pounds a year;
Remote from towns he ran his godly race,
Nor e'er had chang'd, nor wish'd to change his place;
Unskilful he to fawn, or seek for power,
By doctrines fashioned to the varying hour;
Far other aims his heart had learned to prize
More bent to raise the wretched than to rise.
His house was known to all the vagrant train,
He chid their wanderings, but reliev'd their pain;
The long remembered beggar was his guest,
Where beard descending swept his aged breast;
The ruined spendthrift, now no longer proud,
Claimed kindred there, and had his claim allowed;
The broken soldier, kindly bade to stay,
Sat by his fire, and talked the night away;
Wept o'er his wounds, or tales of sorrow done,
Shouldered his crutch, and show'd how fields were won;
Pleased with his guests, the good man learned to glow,
And quite forgot their vices in their woe;
Careless their merits, or their faults to scan,
His pity gave ere charity began.

OLIVER GOLDSMITH (1728-1774)

83

53.   We passed on after we left the forest through many pleasant
       villages until we came near the end of our journey. Then we
began to enquire for the parson at Warfield but no one could tell us
the parson's house or the church, and when we should turn to our
right, they told us to turn to our left. I thought it a very odd place as no
one knew where the parson lived or where the church was, nor did
not know their right hand from their left, many of them. When we got
there, we found no victuals for the horses and an old Irishman told us
it was no use going into the house as there was nothing to be got,
therefore we marched off to the nearest publick house which was a
mile and a half off. We stopt there about two houres and a half and
had some dinner and smoaked a pipe. Went back to the parson's
house and the servants said we aut not to of went away as there was a
good dinner and everything elce for us. He gave me two glasses of
wine and if I could of got hold of the old Irishman, I would of gave
hime two kicks on the rump.

WILLIAM TAYLER (1807—1892)

Wealth

54.   The Squire was a cultivated man of a cultured family with
       many quarterings. He lived in a large house set deep in a very
beautiful park, yet not too deep that it could not be seen in glimpses
from the road, and some portion of its western aspect by reason of a
footpath that skirted a ha-ha which marked the limit of the lawn. The
house or hall, built in the early part of the eighteenth century, was
added to, embellished by a ballroom and picture gallery, together
with outbuildings and water tower, to the certain impoverishment of
the owners. But it had no bathroom. There were, of course, the usual
plethora of servants—housekeeper, cook, kitchen maid, butler,
footman, coachman, valet, upper and under house-maids, maid-of-
all-work, laundry maid, etc.

   The regnant squire when my grandfather was very young was a
Squarson—the Rev. Charles Montagu Doughty, who married
Frederica Beaumont, daughter of the Honourable and Rev.
Frederick Hotham, Rector of Dennington and Prebendary of
Rochester. By several astute marriages the Doughtys had added
wide lands to their estates.

ALLAN JOBSON (1889—1980)

55.   On a grey but dry November morning Dorothea drove to
       Lowick in company with her uncle and Celia. Mr Casaubon's
home was the manor-house. Close by, visible from some parts of the
garden, was the little church, with the old parsonage opposite. In the
beginning of his career, Mr Casaubon had only held the living, but
the death of his brother had put him in possession of the manor also.
It had a small park, with a fine old oak here and there, and an avenue
of limes towards the south-west front, with a sunk fence between
park and pleasure-ground, so that from the drawing room windows
the glance swept uninterruptedly along a slope of greensward till the
limes ended in a level of corn and pastures, which often seemed to
melt into a lake under the setting sun. . . .

   They were soon on a gravel walk which led chiefly between grassy

85

borders and clumps of trees, this being the nearest way to the church, Mr Casaubon said. At the little gate leading into the churchyard there was a pause while Mr Casaubon went to the parsonage close by to fetch a key. . . .

Mr Tucker was the middle-aged curate, one of the 'inferior clergy'. . . . Mr Tucker was invaluable in their walk; and perhaps Mr Casaubon had not been without foresight on this head, the curate being able to answer all Dorothea's questions about the villagers and the other parishioners. Everybody, he assured her, was well off in Lowick: not a cottager in those double cottages at a low rent but kept a pig, and the strips of garden at the back were well tended. The small boys wore excellent corduroy, the girls went out as tidy servants, or did a little straw-plaiting at home: no looms here, no Dissent: and though the public disposition was rather towards laying-by money than towards spirituality, there was not much vice . . . .

Dorothea sank into silence on the way back to the house. She felt some disappointment, of which she was yet ashamed, that there was nothing for her to do in Lowick; and in the next few minutes her mind had glanced over the possibility, which she would have preferred, of finding that her home would be in a parish which had a larger share of the world's misery, so that she might have had more active duties in it . . . .

Mr Tucker soon left them, having some clerical work which would not allow him to lunch at the Hall.

GEORGE ELIOT (1819—1880)

56. *Decbr 1, Sunday*

We breakfasted, dined, &c. again at home. Mr Dade (my curate) called on me this Morning before Divine Service, and I paid him, half a Years serving Weston Church for me, due about this time 15.6.0. Nancy and her Brother went to Church this Morn'. Mr Custance was at Church and he brought them home in his Coach but he did not come in. Dinner to day, Cod-Fish & a Co. Ducks roasted. Bread given to the Poor at Church to day. Wheat being very dear 50 Shillings per Coomb.

86

Decbr 3, Tuesday
We breakfasted, dined, &c. again at home. The Poor complain of the small Quantity of Bread given to them on Sunday at Church almost as much as if they had none given. Dinner to day, Leg of Mutton roasted &c. Nancy's Brother took a ride this Morning to Dr Thorne's at Mattishall, where he dined & spent the Afternoon—returned to Supper &c. I was but poorly all the whole Day.

Decbr 5, Thursday
Dinner to day, Skaite & a Neck of Mutton roasted &c. I was something better thank God! this Day. Sent Ben round the Parish this Morning to give notice of my Tithe-Audit on Tuesday next.

Decbr 9, Monday
We breakfasted, dined, &c. again at home. Mr Maynard called on us this Morning. Busy to day in preparing for my Tithe-Audit to Morrow. Dinner to day, boiled Veal &c.

Decbr 12, Thursday
We breakfasted, dined, &c. again at home. Farmer Hugh Bush of this Parish who has been missing from his House ever since Sunday Afternoon December 1st was this Morning found drowned in a Pond near his House. It is supposed that he destroyed himself. He and Family lived most unhappily. Dinner to day, boiled Beef &c.

Decbr 13, Friday
We breakfasted, dined &c. at home. A Coroner's Inquest was this Morn' taken on the Body of the late Farmer Hugh Bush of this Parish by Colls—Coroner—their Verdict was Lunacy. . . . I had for my Dinner fryed Beef & Cabbage and a Rabbit roasted, &c.

Decbr 15, Sunday
We breakfasted, dined, &c. again at home. Mr Dade read Prayers & Preached this Morn' at Weston Church. Sent Ben this Morn' to Mr Stoughton of Sparham to desire him to administer the H. Sacrament at Weston Church on Christmas Day or the Sunday following

for Mr Dade, as he is not in Priests Orders, which he very kindly sent
me word he would do on the Sunday after Christmas-Day. Dinner to
day, a Turkey roasted &c.

JAMES WOODFORDE (1740—1803)

Poverty

57.   And now, pray, can you solve me the following problem?
Given a man with a wife and six children: let him be obliged always to exhibit himself when outside his own door in a suit of black broadcloth, such as will not undermine the foundations of the Establishment by a paltry plebeian glossiness or an unseemly whiteness at the edges; in a snowy cravat, which is a serious investment of labour in the hemming, starching, and ironing departments; and in a hat which shows no symptom of taking to the hideous doctrine of expediency, and shaping itself according to circumstances; let him have a parish large enough to create an external necessity for abundant shoe-leather, and an internal necessity for abundant beef and mutton, as well as poor enough to require frequent priestly consolation in the shape of shillings and sixpences; and, lastly, let him be compelled, by his own pride and other people's, to dress his wife and children with gentility from bonnet-strings to shoe-strings. By what process of division can the sum of eighty pounds per annum be made to yield a quotient which will cover that man's weekly expenses? This was the problem presented by the position of the Rev. Amos Barton, as curate of Shepperton. . . .
Indeed the equation of income and expenditure was offering new and constantly accumulating difficulties to Mr and Mrs Barton; for shortly after the birth of little Walter, Milly's aunt, who had lived with her ever since her marriage, had withdrawn herself, her furniture, and her yearly income, to the household of another niece; prompted to that step, very probably, by a slight 'tiff' with the Rev. Amos, which occurred while Milly was up-stairs, and proved one too many for the elderly lady's patience and magnanimity. Mr Barton's temper was a little warm, but, on the other hand, elderly maiden ladies are known to be susceptible; so we will not suppose that all the blame lay on his side—the less so, as he had every motive for humouring an inmate whose presence kept the wolf from the door. It was now nearly a year since Miss Jackson's departure, and, to a fine ear, the howl of the wolf was audibly approaching. . . .

Mrs Barton now lighted her candle, and seated herself before her heap of stockings. She had something disagreeable to tell her husband. . . .

'And dear, Woods the butcher called, to say he must have some money next week. He has payment to make up.'

This announcement made Mr Barton thoughtful. He puffed more rapidly, and looked at the fire.

'I think I must ask Hackit to lend me twenty pounds, for it is nearly two months till Lady-day, and we can't give Woods our last shilling.'

'I hardly like you to ask Mr Hackit, dear—he and Mrs Hackit have been so very kind to us; they have sent us so many things lately.'

'Then I must ask Oldinport. I'm going to write to him tomorrow morning. . . .'

'I wish we could do without borrowing money, and yet I don't see how we can. Poor Fred must have some new shoes; I couldn't let him go to Mrs Bond's yesterday because his toes were peeping out, dear child! and I can't let him walk anywhere except in the garden. He must have a pair before Sunday. Really, boots and shoes are the greatest trouble of my life. Everything else one can turn and turn about, and make old look like new; but there's no coaxing boots and shoes to look better than they are.'

GEORGE ELIOT (1819—1880)

58. On her elderly bicycle with the basketwork carrier on the handle-bars, Dorothy free-wheeled down the hill, doing mental arithmetic with three pounds nineteen and fourpence—her entire stock of money until next quarter-day.

She had been through the list of things that were needed in the kitchen. But indeed, was there anything that was *not* needed in the kitchen? Tea, coffee, soap, matches, candles, sugar, lentils, firewood, soda, lamp oil, boot polish, margarine, baking powder— there seemed to be practically nothing that they were not running short of. And at every moment some fresh item that she had forgotten popped up and dismayed her. The laundry bill, for example, and the fact that the coal was running short, and the question of the fish for Friday. The Rector was 'difficult' about fish. Roughly speaking, he would only eat the more expensive kinds; cod, whiting, sprats, skate, herrings, and kippers he refused.

Meanwhile, she had got to settle about the meat for today's dinner—luncheon. (Dorothy was careful to obey her father and call it *luncheon*, when she remembered it. On the other hand, you could not in honesty call the evening meal anything but 'supper'; so there was no such meal as 'dinner' at the Rectory.) Better make an omelette for luncheon today, Dorothy decided. . . . Though, of course, if they had an omelette for luncheon and then scrambled eggs for supper, her father would probably be sarcastic about it. Last time they had had eggs twice in one day, he had inquired coldly, 'Have you started a chicken farm, Dorothy?' And perhaps tomorrow she would get two pounds of sausages at the International, and that staved off the meat-question for one day more.

Thirty-nine further days, with only three pounds nineteen and fourpence to provide for them, loomed up in Dorothy's imagination, sending through her a wave of self-pity which she checked almost instantly. Now then, Dorothy! No snivelling, please! It all comes right somehow if you trust in God. Matthew vi, 25. The Lord will provide. Will he?

GEORGE ORWELL (1903—1950)

59.   That you, friend Marcus, like a stoic,
      Can wish to die in strains heroic,
      No real fortitude implies:
      Yet, all must own, thy wish is wise.
      Thy curate's place, thy fruitful wife,
      Thy busy, drudging scene of life,
      Thy insolent, illiterate vicar,
      Thy want of all-consoling liquor,
      Thy threadbare gown, thy cassock rent,
      Thy credit sunk, thy money spent,
      Thy week made up of fasting-days,
      Thy grate unconscious of a blaze,

And to complete thy other curses,
The quarterly demands of nurses,
Are ills you wisely wish to leave,
And fly for refuge to the grave;
And, O, what virtue you express,
In wishing such afflictions less!

JONATHAN SWIFT (1667—1745)

60.   The tithes, his parish freely paid, he took;
But never sued, or cursed with bell and book.
With patience bearing wrong; but offering none;
Since every man is free to lose his own.
The country churls, according to their kind,
(Who grudge their dues, and love to be behind.)
The less he sought his offering, pinched the more,
And praised a priest contented to be poor.
   Yet of his little he had some to spare,
To feed the famished, and to clothe the bare:
For mortified he was to that degree,
A poorer than himself, he would not see.
True priests, he said, and preachers of the Word,
Were only stewards of their sovereign Lord;
Nothing was theirs; but all the public store:
Entrusted riches, to relieve the poòr.
Who, should they steal, for want of his relief,
He judged himself accomplice with the thief.
   Wide was his parish; not contracted close,
In streets, but here and there a straggling house;
Yet still he was at hand, without request,
To serve the sick; to succour the distressed:
Tempting, on foot, alone without affright,
The dangers of a dark tempestuous night.
   All this the good old man performed alone,
Nor spared his pains; for curate he had none.
Nor durst he trust another with his care;

Nor rode himself to Paul's, the public fair,
To chaffer for preferment with his gold,
Where bishoprics and sinecures are sold.
But duly watched his flock, by night and day;
And from the prowling wolf redeemed the prey;
And hungry sent the wily fox away.

JOHN DRYDEN (1631—1700)

ON THE MARSHES

Sickness and Death

61. I thought I would not let this parcel go without a line or two
     from the parson of the parish, though he has nothing very
material to say, having wrote to you so lately as Saturday last: but it
was well that I took my pen in hand then, for since that time to this
day I should not have been able to have done it, having been
extremely ill with the cholic; on Friday evening I found myself a little
out of order with some twinges and gripings in my bowels, upon
which I had recourse, as usual to a piece of rhubarb, which operated
very well; but whether I caught any cold at that time I know not, but
on Sunday morning about two o'clock I waked in violent pain, and
was obliged to get up to the close stool; but had no relief there; I then
took some pepper mint water, and after some time that took effect,
and brought it to a violent purging, which continued all that day; I
was obliged in the morning to send round the parish to give notice
there would be no service till the afternoon, (though it was a
Sacrament Day) and then got a neighbour to assist me: the
Archdeacon and Mrs Spry came over in the afternoon to see how I
did, and they advised me to take a dose of tincture of rhubarb that
night, which I did, so that I was upon the stool good part of Monday
again; on Tuesday morning I waked early with another motion,
attended with somewhat of piles, which made me very weak and
low; my wife would have me send for our Dr Cooper, which I did, and
he prescribed some proper things for me, which I took yesterday,
and now think myself fine and well, though I have not been out of
doors, nor hardly down stairs till today, since Saturday; tomorrow I
am to take some physic, and that is to be the finishing stroke. I don't
know, that I ever was so much out of order before, except when I was
ill in the West Indies, for I have had a lurking fever about me all this
while, which is now got the better of: today I am to eat some chicken,
for I have had nothing yet but milk porridge and water gruel, which is
but sorry diet for me, who have a tolerable good stroke at a joint of
meat.

GEORGE WOODWARD (1708—1790)

62. My dear Peggy,

And all the rest of my dear children, may the watchful Providence of Almighty God keep you ever under his Protection! You see, my dears, I am still able write you: and I do not know, that I can so well, surely not so agreeably, use that ability. God is very good to me, and my Gout seems walking off. I am able to rise from the Chair, and walk the Room a few Turns by the Help of a Stick, which your Mamma this morning bought at a Toy Shop, and made me a Present of. The Doctor has altered my Regimen: I am now to take Water from the Cross Bath at 7 and 8 o'clock mornings, and from the King's Bath at 12, quarter a Pint each time. Every one, who comes in, tells me this exactness as to Time and Quantity is a mere Farce, notwithstanding the Doctors so gravely prescribe: and it may be so for aught I know; but as it may not be so, I'll try stricktly adhere to Rule. Some say, the Waters heat them; some, that they make them giddy; others talk of other Effects from them: I can only say, that I have no Effect, which I know of, from drinking the Water, but that it quenches my Thirst, which at present is an excellent Quality in it, for I have been thirsty, more or less, almost from the Beginning of my Journey. As my Gout goes off, my Thirst will abate, and I think it is not near so great as it was a day or two ago.

JOHN PENROSE (1712—1776)

63. Miss Ward, at the end of half a dozen years, found herself obliged to be attached to the Rev. Mr Norris, a friend of her brother-in-law, Sir Thomas Bertram of Mansfield Park, with scarcely any private fortune. . . . Miss Ward's match, indeed, when it came to the point was not contemptible, Sir Thomas being happily able to give his friend an income in the living of Mansfield, and Mr and Mrs Norris began their career of conjugal felicity with little less than a thousand a year. . . .

The first event of any importance in the family was the death of Mr Norris, which happened when Fanny was about fifteen, and necessarily introduced alterations and novelties. Mrs Norris, on quitting the parsonage, removed first to the park, and afterwards to a small house of Sir Thomas's in the village, and consoled herself for the loss of her husband by considering that she could do very well without him, and for her reduction in income by the evident necessity of stricter economy.

JANE AUSTEN (1775—1817)

64.   When old Mr Gilfil died, thirty years ago, there was general sorrow in Shepperton; and if black cloth had not been hung round the pulpit and reading-desk, by order of his nephew and principal legatee, the parishioners would certainly have subscribed the necessary sum out of their own pockets, rather than allow such a tribute of respect to be wanting. All the farmers' wives brought out their black bombasines; and Mrs Jennings, at the Wharf, by appearing the first Sunday after Mr Gilfil's death in her salmon-coloured ribbons and green shawl, excited the severest remark. To be sure, Mrs Jennings was a new-comer, and town-bred, so that she could hardly be expected to have very clear notions of what was proper; but, as Mrs Higgins observed in an undertone to Mrs Parrot when they were coming out of church, 'Her husband, who'd been born i' the parish, might ha' told her better. . . .'

Even dirty Dame Fripp, who was a very rare church-goer, had been to Mrs Hackit to beg a bit of old crape, and with this sign of grief pinned on her little coal-scuttle bonnet, was seen dropping her curtsy opposite the reading-desk.

GEORGE ELIOT (1819—1880)

65.   The first sight of the Rapstone Valley is of something unexpectedly isolated and uninterruptedly rural; a solitary jogger is the only outward sign of urban pollution. . . . There were an unusual number of cars parked in front of the Rectory and round the churchyard, and there was a small clutch of reporters and a couple of press photographers on the day of the Rector's funeral, for Simeon Simcox had, in his life time, achieved a fame, some would say a notoriety, which stretched far beyond the boundaries of his parish.

97

'We brought nothing into this world, and it is certain we can carry nothing out,' said the Reverend Kevin Bulstrode, Vicar of Skurfield, conducting the service in the unavoidable absence of the Rector of Rapstone.

'*Naked* come I out of my mother's womb, and naked *shall* I return thither,' a furious and gravelly whisper came from the congregation. The Vicar of Skurfield, who would shortly take over Rapstone also when the parishes were amalgamated under a new scheme of 'rationalisation', did his best to ignore the interruption. 'The Lord gives and the Lord takes away, blessed be the name of the Lord,' he continued bravely. . . .

'Shush, Henry,' his wife Lonnie, sitting beside him, had whispered nervously when he interrupted the Vicar, but Henry grumbled to himself, 'Why should the Reverend Trendy Kev get away with castrating the prayer-book?. . .'

Fred Simcox and his mother were whispering together as the Reverend Kevin Bulstrode climbed into the pulpit. . . . 'For Simeon Simcox,' Bulstrode was saying, 'the Church of England wasn't the Establishment at prayer, it was the force of progress on the march. One of the many obituaries in the national press suggests that he may have been a bit of a saint. If so, he was a saint smoking a pipe, dressed in that old tweed jacket with leather patches we came to love and know so well, a very caring sort of saint, be it at the Worsfield Missile Base or leading us in prayer outside the South African High Commission. . . . One of his parishioners, our old friend "Peasticks" Bigwell, must have the last word. "He were a smasher, our old Rector, weren't he?" Peasticks said to me. Well, perhaps it wasn't the description we'd all use.'

'Hardly,' Henry whispered to Lonnie, 'for a dedicated pacifist'.

'But, you know, I think Simeon would have understood. Today we are gathered together to say goodbye to a "smasher".'

After the funeral service many of the congregation, some starting to chatter, others lighting cigarettes, all relieved that the worst was over, crowded into the Rectory. . . . The Rural Dean was doing his best, on the minute glass of sherry provided, to make the party go. . . . He recalled how very famous Simeon Simcox had been.

'Not a conventional clergyman, of course. The Bishop had to haul him over the coals when he was getting too deeply into politics. Saints are never the easiest of people to get along with. You put that across jolly well, Kevin.'

'Thank you.' Bulstrode was gratified. 'I think we managed to strike just the right note of reverent informality.' Unfortunately he was within earshot of Henry, who came delightedly in on the cue.

'I think you struck a perfectly ghastly note. That castrated edition of the prayer-book may be perfectly suitable to bless the union of a couple of crimpers in a unisex hairdo establishment. It's got no place in the Christian burial of a priest of the Church of England.'

JOHN MORTIMER (1921—)

66.   Of no class of men can it be more truly said that the good they do dies with them, and the evil lives—in the memory of men—than the country parson. Of the thousands of old rectors and vicars of past generations, how they have all slipped out of the memory of men, have left no tradition whatever behind them, if they were good! But the few bad ones did so impress themselves on their generation, that the stories of their misconduct have been handed on, and are not forgotten in a century . . . .

In my own parish in which I was reared, Romaine, one of the most brilliant luminaries of the evangelical revival, acted as curate for a while, but not the smallest trace of any tradition of his goodness, his eloquence, his zeal did I discover among the villagers. At the very time that Romaine was in this parish, there was a curate in an adjoining one who was over-fond of the bottle, and was picked up out of the ditch on more than one occasion. Neither his name nor his delinquencies are forgotten to this day.

S. BARING GOULD (1832—1924)

PARISH CHURCH

3. AT CHURCH

Church building

67. 'Eh, dear,' said Mrs Patten, falling back in her chair, and lifting
     up her little withered hands, 'what 'ud Mr Gilfil say, if he was
worthy to know the changes as have come about i' the Church these
last ten years? I don't understand these new sort o' doctrines. . . . But
it's well for me as I can't go to church any longer, for if th' old singers
are to be done away with, there'll be nothing left as it was in Mr
Patten's time; and what's more, I hear you've settled to pull the
church down and build it up new?'
   Now the fact was that the Rev. Amos Barton, on his last visit to Mrs
Patten, had urged her to enlarge her promised subscription of
twenty pounds, representing to her that she was only a steward of
her riches, and that she could not spend them more for the glory of
God than by giving a heavy subscription towards the rebuilding of
Shepperton Church—a practical precept which was not likely to
smooth the way to her acceptance of his theological doctrine. Mr
Hackit. . . was glad of the new turn given to the subject by this
question, addressed to him as church-warden and an authority in all
parochial matters.
   'Ah,' he answered, 'the parson's bothered us into it at last, and
we're to begin pulling down this spring. But we haven't got money
enough yet. I was for waiting till we'd made up the sum, and, for my
part, I think the congregation's fell off o' late; though Mr Barton says
that's because there's been no room for the people when they've
come. You see, the congregation got so large in Parry's time, the

people stood in the aisles; but there's never any crowd now, as I can
see.'

GEORGE ELIOT (1819—1880)

68.   On his arrival in Meadenham, Mr Harvey had discovered that
      the fabric of Saint Matthew Without was in poor repair. There
was a great deal of work needing doing, particularly on the roof.
Believing himself the sole controller of the parish, he had decided to
sell off some of the church's small amount of silver to help pay for the
roof and for the other structural work, but the decision had spilt the
village and caused a great deal of ill-feeling. There was talk of a con-
sistory court and he was called to discuss the matter with his bishop.

Who counselled him to bend with the wind rather than being stiff-
necked and breaking. Difficult advice from a younger man to a priest
who was in his sixty-second year of life and his fortieth year of
ministry.

But Barton Harvey took the advice and his parish had been a
better and happier place for it. The congregation had fallen from an
average of thirty-four to twenty-five during those awkward months.
Now they had picked up again, as spring advanced, to twenty-nine.

But the roof was still in a sorry state.

Seeburg's of Nazebury had quoted a total of eleven thousand
three hundred and forty-five pounds—including VAT—to do the
work and the appeal fund was still an almost impossible distance
from that target.

So Barton Harvey had got together with Father McLaglen from
the Catholic church and they had agreed that they would devote
much of their energies during the year to raising money. Saint
Michael's was by no means a wealthy church and they had also
agreed that they would divide the money between them. This agreement had come with some reluctance from the Reverend Harvey,
who felt that his need was somewhat the greater.

MARY FRASER

102

69.   Dorothy stopped and got off her bicycle.

'Beg pardon, Miss,' said Proggett. 'I been wanting to speak to you, Miss—*partic'lar*.'

Dorothy sighed inwardly. When Proggett wanted to speak to you *partic'lar*, you could be perfectly certain what was coming; it was some piece of alarming news about the condition of the church. Proggett was a pessimistic, conscientious man, and a very loyal churchman, after his fashion. Too dim of intellect to have any definite religious beliefs, he showed his piety by an intense solicitude about the state of the church buildings. . . .

'What is it, Proggett?' said Dorothy.

'Well, Miss, it's they . . . bells. . . . They bells up in the church tower. They're a-splintering through that there belfry floor in a way as it makes you fair shudder to look at 'em. We'll have 'em down atop of us before we know where we are. I was up the belfry 'smorning, and I tell you I come down faster'n I went up, when I saw how that there floor's a-busting underneath 'em.'

Proggett came to complain about the condition of the bells not less than once in a fortnight. It was now three years that they had been lying on the floor of the belfry, because the cost of either reswinging or removing them was estimated at twenty-five pounds, which might as well have been twenty-five thousand for all the chance there was of paying it. They were really almost as dangerous as Proggett made out. It was quite certain that, if not this year or next, at any rate at some time in the near future, they would fall through the belfry floor into the church porch. And, as Proggett was fond of pointing out, it would probably happen on a Sunday morning just as the congregation were coming into church.

Dorothy sighed again. Those wretched bells were never out of mind for long; there were times when the thought of their falling even got into her dreams. There was always some trouble or other at the church. If it was not the belfry, then it was the roof or the walls; or it was a broken pew which the carpenter wanted ten shillings to mend; or it was seven hymn-books needed at one and sixpence each, or the flue of the stove choked up—and the sweep's fee was half a crown— or a smashed window-pane or the choir-boys' cassocks in rags.

There was never enough money for anything. The new organ which the Rector had insisted on buying five years earlier—the old one, he said, reminded him of a cow with the asthma—was a burden under which the Church Expenses fund had been staggering ever since.

'I don't know *what* we can do,' said Dorothy finally; 'I really don't. We've simply no money at all. And even if we do make anything out of the school-children's play, it's all got to go to the organ fund. The organ people are really getting quite nasty about their bill. Have you spoken to my father?'

'Yes, Miss. He don't make nothing of it. "Belfry's held up five hundred years," he says; "we can trust it to hold up a few years longer." '

This was quite according to precedent. The fact that the church was visibly collapsing over his head made no impression on the Rector; he simply ignored it, as he ignored anything else that he did not wish to be worried about.

GEORGE ORWELL (1903—1950)

70.   In the parish church of Crome Mr Bodiham preached on 1 Kings vi. 18: 'And the cedar of the house within was carved with knops'—a sermon of immediate local interest. For the past two years the problem of the War Memorial had exercised the minds of all those in Crome who had enough leisure, or mental energy, or party spirit to think of such things. Henry Wimbush was all for a library—a library of local literature, stocked with county histories, old maps of the district, monographs on the local antiquities, dialect dictionaries, handbooks of the local geology and natural history. He liked to think of the villagers, inspired by such reading, making up parties of a Sunday afternoon to look for fossils and flint arrow-heads. The villagers themselves favoured the idea of a memorial reservoir and water supply. But the busiest and most articulate party followed Mr Bodiham in demanding something religious in character—a second lich-gate, for example, a stained-glass window, a monument of marble, or, if possible, all three. So far, however, nothing had been done, partly because the memorial committee had never been able to agree, partly for the more cogent reason that

104

too little money had been subscribed to carry out any of the proposed schemes. Every three or four months Mr Bodiham preached a sermon on the subject. His last had been delivered in March; it was high time that his congregation had a fresh reminder.

'And the cedar of the house within was carved with knops.'

Mr Bodiham touched lightly on Solomon's temple. From thence he passed to temples and churches in general. What were the characteristics of these buildings dedicated to God? Obviously, the fact of their, from a human point of view, complete uselessness. They were unpractical buildings 'carved with knops.' Solomon might have built a library—indeed, what could be more to the taste of the world's wisest man? He might have dug a reservoir—what more useful in a parched city like Jerusalem? He did neither; he built a house all carved with knops, useless and unpractical. Why? Because he was dedicating the work to God. There had been much talk in Crome about the proposed War Memorial. A War Memorial was, in its very nature, a work dedicated to God. . . . A library, a reservoir? Mr Bodiham scornfully and indignantly condemnded the idea. These were works dedicated to man, not to God. As a War Memorial they were totally unsuitable. A lich-gate had been suggested. This was an object which answered perfectly to the definition of a War Memorial: a useless work dedicated to God and carved with knops. One lich-gate, it was true, already existed. But nothing would be easier than to make a second entrance into the churchyard; and a second entrance would need a second gate. . . .

Henry Wimbush walked home thinking of the books he would present to the War Memorial Library, if ever it came into existence.

ALDOUS HUXLEY (1894—1963)

Sunday Services

71. Bleadon, as a parish Church is a good building, but rendered
      cold and wretched to the eye by neglect and nakedness....
The interior of the Church, was quite as cheerless to my mind as
the exterior—bare, and cold, and dreary.... The Rev. David
Williams was in the reading-desk when I entered, going through the
service, just as you would suppose the service to be gone through in
such a church as I have described. He seemed to be suffering from
flatulency, for at every other verse he was obliged to pause,
afterwards wiping his mouth with an old brown handkerchief, and
occasionally varying the act by using the sleeve of his surplice (which
was far from clean) for the purpose. There was no singing or musical
service whatever, the Rev. Gentleman objecting to it, as I have
heard, on the grounds that it affects his head, but he has never
complained of it affecting his heart. On some occasions, however,
the Uphill singers have come over, and been permitted to 'perform;'
but not very long since, being rather too energetic in their exertions,
they were publicly, and from what little I know of country choirs,
perhaps justly, rebuked by the Rector for their overpowering
vocalism.—'If you can't sing better,' said he, 'don't sing at all—shut
up that noise!' This familiar and almost household mode of censure
is not very unfrequent, however, at Bleadon; he has occasionally
paused in the midst of the Psalms, to correct the clerk for reading too
fast or too loud, but by way of reprisals the clerk has sometimes had
to correct the parson for reading the wrong psalm, an incident of this
kind having occurred, I think, on Whitsunday last....
The worshippers were few, and the worship cold. The priest
delivered his part in a tone of apathy and the replies of the people
were faint and languid; the reading of the clergyman was not good,
that of the poor clerk barbarous.

JOSEPH LEECH (1815—1893)

72. The Rev. John Lewis Bythesea, LL.B., was Rector of
      Bagendon from 1800 till 1845.... In his old age, before he

had realized the necessity of getting assistance, he was in the habit of getting the young lad Dick to go to the Church before afternoon service with a bag of sixpences, and these were his directions: 'Stand in the porch, and if any woman comes, say "the Rector does not want to be at Church this afternoon—but if you go in he'll come." ' The transaction that took place may be imagined, and it will also be surmised that there was a greater and still greater drain upon the bag, as time went on and the situation became noised abroad.

GEORGE EDWARD REES (1854—1945)

73.   In other churches I have observed, that nothing unseemly or ruinous is to be found, except in the clergyman, and the appendages of his person. The squire of the parish, or his ancestors ... have adorned the altar-piece with the richest crimson velvet, embroidered with vine leaves and ears of wheat; and have dressed up the pulpit with the same splendour and expense; while the gentleman, who fills it, is exalted in the midst of all this finery, with a surplice as dirty as a farmer's frock, and a periwig that seems to have transferred its faculty of curling to the band which appears in full buckle beneath it.

But if I was concerned to see several distressed pastors, as well as many of our country churches, in a tottering condition, I was more offended with the indecency of worship in others. I could wish that the clergy would inform their congregations, that there is no occasion to scream themselves hoarse in making the responses; that the town-crier is not the only person qualified to pray with due devotion; and that he who bawls the loudest may nevertheless be the wickedest fellow in the parish. The old women too in the aisle might be told, that their time would be better employed in attending to the sermon, than in fumbling over their tattered testaments till they have found the text; by which time the discourse is near drawing to a conclusion: while a word or two of instruction might not be thrown away upon the younger part of the congregation, to teach them that making posies in summer time, and cracking nuts in autumn is no part of the religious ceremony.

WILLIAM COWPER (1731—1800)

107

74. *Easter Sunday, April Eve, 1872*

A soft warm spring morning of changing sunshine and shower. I never was so hard put to it as in Church this morning to resist untimely and inextinguishable laughter. It was almost irresistible. The sun was beating fiercely through the southern windows upon the heads and books of the devout Hodgson party in the Cabalva seat. Mrs Chinnock tried to draw down the blind, but the blind was broken and would not draw or be drawn. Mrs Venables then signed to the clerk to come and pull the blind down. The little man came and pulled and pulled till at last with a more violent tug smash went the wooden bar with a loud report and hung in ruins in the air with a broken back. I knew the crash was coming when I saw the clerk pulling, and when it came it was almost too much. I was nearly choked. There came into my mind suddenly my Father's old story of the clergyman waiting for the hymn before the sermon to be finished and meanwhile looking through the church window and seeing an old woman pulling up a stubborn carrot. At last up came the carrot all at once, over went the old woman on her back head over heels. 'I thought so!' exclaimed the delighted clergyman aloud, to the astonishment of the expectant congregation who had finished the hymn and were waiting for him to begin the prayer.

FRANCIS KILVERT (1840—1872)

75. My choirgirl friend . . . said the vicar was one of those who like to show how broadminded they are by working regardlessly through almost every hymn in the book—and some outside as well. And the choir was one of those who only know about a dozen tunes which have been handed down from generation to generation, and strongly object to learning anything else. Consequently a most keen and enjoyable contest had developed between the vicar and the organist. The vicar would dig up an unknown hymn, and the organist would endeavour to fit it to one of the choir's accepted tunes. The organist and choir had never been beaten, but once they had been in grave danger of losing a point. The vicar had discovered a hymn written in such an extraordinary metre that it refused to be married off to an eligible tune.

Things looked black, and it became obvious that the choir would
have to do the unthinkable and learn a new tune. However, at the
last moment, the vicar was taken ill with 'flu, and a relieving priest
had been prevailed upon to substitute 'Onward, Christian Soldiers.'
REGINAL FRARY (1920—   )

76.   For a couple of years before death divorced him from his parochial charge, the Rev. Samuel Seyer had grown too feeble to
get through the service without some refreshment; and I recollect
full well, just before going up into the pulpit to preach, he used
invariably to walk across to the pew in which an elderly lady, his
sister-in-law, sat . . . and receive from her hands a little lump of sugar,
saturated with some drops of brandy. Good old times those were; no
one wondered, no one made a remark, and the little congregation, a
dozen in number, looked as regularly for parson Seyer's soaked
lump of saccharine as they did for the bidding prayer; though, I
confess, to me, for the first time, it had rather a curious effect, to see
the old man walk across in his canonicals and hold his hand over the
pew for his dole, while the worthy old soul within drew a little phial of
Cognac from one pocket, and deliberately, drop by drop, let the due
quantity fall on the fragment of white sugar which she took from the
other. The Rev. historian having obtained his refresher, proceeded
to mount the pulpit stairs, and as he did, 'munched, and munched,
and munched,' like the sailor's wife in Macbeth, his vivifying morsel.
JOSEPH LEECH (1815—1893)

77.   *A Raw Young Preacher*: His collections of study are the notes
        of sermons, which, taken up at St Mary's, he utters in the coun-
try. . . . His writing is more than his reading, for he reads only what he
gets without book. Thus accomplished he comes down to his
friends, and his first salutation is grace and peace out of the pulpit.
His prayer is conceited, and no man remembers his college more at
large. The pace of his sermon is a full career, and he runs wildly over
hill and dale, till the clock stops him. The labour of it is chiefly in his
lungs. . . . He takes on against the pope without mercy. . . . He
preaches heresy, if it comes his way, though with a mind, I must
needs say, very orthodox. His action is all passion and his speech
interjections. He has an excellent faculty in bemoaning the people,
and spits with a very good grace. . . . He preaches but once a year,
though twice on Sunday; for the stuff is still the same, only the dressing a little altered: he has more tricks with a sermon, than a tailor with
an old cloak, to turn it, and piece it, and at last quite disguise it with a
new preface.

JOHN EARLE (1601—1665)

78.   The parson gave us a most erudite sermon on the rites and
        ceremonies of Christmas, and the propriety of observing it not
merely as a day of thanksgiving, but of rejoicing; supporting the
correctness of his opinions by the earliest usages of the Church, and
enforcing them by the authorities of Theophilus of Casearea, St
Cyprian, St Chrysostom, St Augustine and a cloud more of saints
and Fathers from whom he made copious quotations. I was a little at
a loss to perceive the necessity of such a mighty array of forces to
maintain a point which no one present seemed inclined to dispute;
but I soon found that the good man had a legion of ideal adversaries
to contend with; having in the course of his researches on the subject
of Christmas got completely embroiled in the sectarian
controversies of the Revolution when the Puritans made such a
fierce assault upon the ceremonies of the Church, and poor old

Christmas was driven out of the land by proclamation of parliament. The worthy parson lived but with times past, and knew but a little of the present.

WASHINGTON IRVING (1783—1859)

79.   The vicar climbed, with some effort, into the pulpit. He was an elderly man who had served in India most of his life. . . . He had a noble and sonorous voice and was reckoned the best preacher for many miles around.

His sermons had been composed in his more active days for delivery at the garrison chapel; he had done nothing to adapt them to the changed conditions of his ministry and they mostly concluded with some reference to homes and dear ones far away. The villagers did not find this in any way surprising. Few of the things said in church seemed to have any particular reference to themselves. They enjoyed their vicar's sermons very much and they knew that when he began about their distant homes, it was time to be dusting their knees and feeling for their umbrellas. . . .

That Christmas the vicar preached his usual Christmas sermon. It was one to which his parishioners were greatly attached.

'How difficult it is for us,' he began, blandly surveying his congregation, who coughed into their mufflers and chafed their chilblains under their woollen gloves, 'to realise that this is indeed Christmas. Instead of glowing log fire and windows tight shuttered against the drifting snow, we have only the harsh glare of an alien sun; instead of the happy circle of loved faces, of home and family, we have the uncomprehending stares of the subjugated, though no doubt grateful, heathen. Instead of the placid ox and ass of Bethlehem,' said the vicar, slightly losing the thread of his comparisons, 'we have for companions the ravening tiger and the exotic camel, the furtive jackal and the ponderous elephant. . .' And so on, through the pages of faded manuscript. The words had temporarily touched the heart of many an obdurate trooper, and hearing them again, as he had heard them year after year since Mr Tendril had come to the parish, Tony and most of Tony's guests felt that it was an integral part of their

111

Christmas festivities; one with which they would find it very hard to dispense. 'The ravening tiger and the exotic camel' had long been bywords in the family, of frequent recurrence in all their games.

EVELYN WAUGH (1903—1966)

80. As a preacher, the Rev. Walter Stelling meant always to preach in a striking manner, so as to have his congregation swelled by admirers from neighbouring parishes, and to produce a great sensation whenever he took occasional duty for a brother clergyman of minor gifts. The style of preaching he had chosen was the extemporaneous, which was held little short of the miraculous in rural parishes like King's Lorton. Some passages of Massillon and Bourdaloue, which he knew by heart, were really very effective when rolled out in Mr Stelling's deepest tones; but as comparatively feeble appeals of his own were delivered in the same loud and impressive manner, they were often thought quite as striking by his hearers. Mr Stelling's doctrine was of no particular school; if anything, it had a tinge of evangelicalism, for that was 'the telling thing' just then in the diocese to which King's Lorton belonged.

GEORGE ELIOT (1819—1880)

81. There was excitement in the parish of Narrobourne one day. The congregation had just come out from morning service, and the whole conversation was of the new curate, Mr Halborough, who had officiated for the first time, in the absence of the rector.

Never before had the feelings of the villagers approached a level which could be called excitement on such a matter as this. The droning which had been the rule in that quiet old place for a century seemed ended at last. They repeated the text to each other as a refrain: 'O Lord, be thou my helper!' Not within living memory till today had the subject of the sermon formed the topic of conversation from the church door to the churchyard gate, to the exclusion of personal remarks on those who had been present, and on the week's news in general.

112

The thrilling periods of the preacher hung about their minds all that day. The parish being steeped in indifferentism, it happened that when the youths and maidens, middle-aged and old people, who had attended church that morning, recurred as by a fascination to what Halborough had said, they did so more or less indirectly, and even with the subterfuge of a light laugh that was not real, so great was their shyness under the novelty of their sensations.

What was more curious than that these unconventional villagers should have been excited by a preacher of a new school after forty years of familiarity with the old hand who had had charge of their souls, was the effect of Halborough's address upon the occupants of the manor-house pew, including the owner of the estate. These thought they knew how to discount the mere sensational sermon, how to minimize flash oratory to its bare proportions; but they had yielded like the rest of the assembly to the charm of the newcomer.

THOMAS HARDY (1840—1928)

82.　'It's like this, Bertie,' said Eustace, settling down cosily. 'As I told you in my letter, there are nine of us marooned in this desert spot, reading with old Heppenstall. Well, of course, nothing is jollier than sweating up the Classics when it's a hundred in the shade, but there does come a time when you begin to feel the need of a little relaxation; and, by Jove, there are absolutely no facilities for relaxation in this place whatever. And then Steggles got this idea. Steggles is one of our reading-party....'

'What idea?'

'Well, you know how many parsons there are round about here. There are about a dozen hamlets within a radius of six miles, and each hamlet has a church and each church has a parson and each parson preaches a sermon every Sunday. Tomorrow week— Sunday the twenty-third—we're running off the great Sermon Handicap. Steggles is making the book. Each parson is to be clocked by a reliable steward of the course, and the one that preaches the longest sermon wins. Did you study the race-card I sent you?'

'I couldn't understand what it was all about.'

113

'Why, you chump, it gives the handicaps and the current odds on each starter....'

'Why, it's a sitter for old Heppenstall,' I said. 'He's got the event sewed up in a parcel. There isn't a parson in the land who could give him eight minutes. Your pal Steggles must be an ass, giving him a handicap like that. Why, in the days when I was with him, old Heppenstall never used to preach under half an hour, and there was one sermon of his on Brotherly Love which lasted forty-five minutes if it lasted a second. Has he lost his vim lately, or what is it?'

'Not a bit of it,' said Eustace. 'Tell him what happened, Claude.'

'Why,' said Claude, 'the first Sunday we were here, we all went to Twing church, and old Heppenstall preached a sermon that was well under twenty minutes. This is what happened. Steggles didn't notice it, and the Rev. didn't notice it himself, but Eustace and I both spotted that he dropped a chunk of at least half-a-dozen pages out of his sermon-case as he was walking up to the pulpit. He sort of flickered when he got to the gap in the manuscript, but carried on all right, and Steggles went away with the impression that twenty minutes or a bit under was his usual form. The next Sunday we heard Tucker and Starkie, and they both went on well over the thirty-five minutes, so Steggles arranged the handicapping as you see on the card.... But Eustace and I happened by the merest fluke to be riding through Lower Bingley this morning, and there was a wedding on at the church, and it suddenly struck us that it wouldn't be a bad move to get a line on G. Hayward's form, in case he might be a dark horse.'

'And it was jolly lucky we did,' said Eustace. 'He delivered an address of twenty-six minutes by Claude's stop-watch. At a village wedding, mark you! What'll he do when he really extends himself...!'

Not being one of the official stewards, I had my choice of churches..., and naturally I didn't hesitate. The only drawback of going to Lower Bingley was that it was ten miles away, which meant an early start, but I borrowed a bicycle from one of the grooms and tooled off. I had only Eustace's word for it that G. Hayward was such a stayer, and it might have been that he showed too flattering form at that wedding where the twins had heard him preach; but any misgivings I may have had disappeared the moment he got into the pulpit. Eustace had been right. The man was a trier. He was a tall, rangy-looking greybeard, and he went off from the start with a nice, easy action, pausing and clearing his throat at the end of each sentence, and it wasn't five minutes before I realized that here was the winner. His habit of stopping dead and looking round the church at intervals was worth minutes to us, and in the home stretch we gained no little advantage owing to his dropping his pince-nez and having to grope for them. At the twenty-minute mark he had merely settled down. Twenty-five minutes saw him going strong. And when he finally finished with a good burst, the clock showed thirty-five minutes fourteen seconds. With the handicap which he had been given, this seemed to me to make the event easy for him, and it was with much *bonhomie* and goodwill to all men that I hopped on to the old bike and started back to the Hall for lunch.

Bingo was talking on the 'phone when I arrived.

'Fine! Splendid! Topping!' he was saying. 'Eh? Oh, we needn't worry about him. Right-o, I'll tell Bertie.' He hung up the receiver and caught sight of me. 'Oh, hello, Bertie; I was just talking to Eustace. It's all right, old man. The report from Lower Bingley has just got in. G. Hayward romps home.'

'I knew he would. I've just come from there.'

'Oh, were you there? I went to Badgwick. Tucker ran a splendid race, but the handicap was too much for him. Starkie had a sore throat and was nowhere. Roberts, of Fale-by-the-Water, ran third. Good old G. Hayward!' said Bingo, affectionately, and we strolled out on to the terrace.

'Are all the returns in, then?' I asked.

'All except Gandle-by-the-Hill. But we needn't worry about Bates. He never had a chance.'

P.G. WODEHOUSE (1881—1975)

Weddings

83.   Had a wedding but the clerk did not give me notice the day
      before which made me angry. Sunday is a bad day for these
things as it hurries me and I scarce get myself ready for Prayers. It
seems the persons were but lately come to live into the parish and
they had lived together before and they brought a bouncing child to
be christened the very day of their wedding. I gave them a good
jubation and told them that had I known there were such people in
my parish I would not have suffered them to have remained long in
that situation. This they were aware of and so came to be married. I
had not much time in the Sunday School.

WILLIAM HOLLAND (1746—1819)

84.   Rode to Ringland this morning and married one Robert Astick
      and Elizabeth Howlett by licence, Mr Carter being from home,
and the man being in custody, the woman being with child by him.
The man was a long time before he could be prevailed on to marry
her when in the church yard; and at the altar behaved very
unbecoming. It is a cruel thing that any person should be compelled
by law to marry. I received of the officers for marrying them ten
shillings and six pence. It is very disagreeable to me to marry such
persons.

JAMES WOODFORD (1740—1803)

85.   On a week-day morning a small congregation, consisting
      mainly of women and girls, rose from its knees in the mouldy
nave of a church called All Saints'. . . . at the end of a service without
a sermon. They were about to disperse when a smart footstep,
entering the porch and coming up the central passage, arrested their
attention. . . . Everybody looked. A young cavalry soldier in a red
uniform, with the three chevrons of a sergeant upon his sleeve,
strode up the aisle, with an embarrassment which was only the more
marked by the intense vigour of his step, and by the determination
upon his face to show none. . . . Passing on through the chancel
arch, he never paused till he came close to the altar railing. Here for a
moment he stood alone.

116

Baptisms

86.   When the Rev. Candy finally emerged from the vestry he got
       the immediate impression that there were far more people
gathered about the christening font, on which a number of candles
were burning, than he or the Rev. Spinks ever saw at a service. . . .

'Good morning to you all,' the Rev. Candy said. . . . 'Has everyone
his or her little book giving the form of service? And is everyone now
familiar with the batting order?'

'Little Blenheim's first,' Ma said.

'Who is to be the god-parent of this child?'

Angela Snow said she was and succeeded, as she stepped
forward a pace, in looking ravishingly demure.

'Oscar Larkin is next, I believe. Who is the god-parent of this
child?'

'I. Mademoiselle Dupont.'

'Step this way, please.'

Angela Snow, Mademoiselle Dupont and the Rev. Candy retired
some distance from the font and went for some moments into
solemn conclave. . . .

The service presently began. Little Blenheim, being not only very
tiny but also fast asleep, presented no difficulty and lay sweetly
swaddled and oblivious in Mr Candy's arms while Mr Candy poured
unnecessarily large quantities of water over the back of his minute
bald head, so that Ma was quite disgusted and said under her breath:

'Here, don't drown the child in the drink, for goodness' sake.'

Mercifully Mr Candy didn't drown little Blenheim in the drink but
gave him back to Mariette and then turned his attention to little
Oscar. Little Oscar, not by any means all that little now, was a great
weight in his arms. Mr Candy could hardly hold him. Oscar was also
very restless and with his red cherubic face looking not at all unlike a
slightly inebriated piglet struggling about.

'I baptize this child Oscar Columbus Septimus Dupont,' Mr Candy
said, hoping to heaven that he had the names right and at the same
time slopping more unnecessarily large quantities of water over
Oscar's head.

117

The officiating curate, who had not yet doffed his surplice, perceived the new-comer, and followed him to the communion-space.
He whispered to the soldier, and then beckoned to the clerk, who in
his turn whispered to an elderly woman, apparently his wife, and
they also went up the chancel steps.

' 'Tis a wedding!' murmured some of the women, brightening.
'Let's wait!'

The majority sat down.

There was a creaking of machinery behind, and some of the
young ones turned their heads. From the interior face of the west
wall of the tower projected a little canopy with a quarter-jack and
small bell beneath it. . . . The jack had struck half-past eleven.

'Where's the woman?' whispered some of the spectators. . . .

The silence grew to be a noticeable thing as the minutes went on,
and nobody else appeared, and not a soul moved. The rattle of the
quarter-jack again from its niche, its blows for three-quarters, its
fussy retreat, were almost painfully abrupt, and caused many of the
congregation to start palpably.

'I wonder where the woman is!' a voice whispered again.

There began now that slight shifting of feet, that artificial coughing
among several, which betrays a nervous suspense. At length there
was a titter. But the soldier never moved. . . .

The clock ticked on. The women threw off their nervousness, and
titters and giggling became more frequent. Then came a dead
silence. . . . The rattle began again, the puppet emerged, and the
four quarters were struck fitfully as before. . . . Then followed the
dull and remote resonance of the twelve heavy strokes in the tower
above. The women were impressed, and there was no giggle this
time.

The clergyman glided into the vestry, and the clerk vanished. The
sergeant had not yet turned; every woman in church was waiting to
see his face, and he appeared to know it. At last he did turn, and
stalked resolutely down the nave, braving them all, with a com-
pressed lip.

THOMAS HARDY (1840—1926)

118

Almost immediately afterwards Oscar, who had insisted on bringing Ma's wooden spoon to church with him—and why not? Ma said, if it would keep the child pacified—struck Mr Candy a severe blow on the top of the head with it. . . .

'Here, give him back to me,' Ma said and Mr Candy promptly did so, with undisguised relief and a faint smile that seemed to indicate that he was quite used to this sort of thing.

Instantly Oscar, rudely deprived of the pleasure of using Mr Candy's head as a drum, burst loudly into tears, with the result that Ma had hastily to take him out of church. . . .

Confused by the unexpected attack on him, Mr Candy now discovered that he had forgotten the batting order. . . .

The result of this was that he called Montgomery next and Montgomery, being covered in adolescent masculine shyness as opposed to the serene aplomb of the girls, hastily stepped forward, only too glad to get the ordeal over. He was shortly followed by Mariette, who treated the occasion with such grace and dignity, together with a complete detachment. . . .

Some knowledge of the batting order was now essential because of the twins. That simply had to be right and Mr Candy hastily refreshed his memory about their names and ribbon colours. Zinnia would be wearing the red ribbon and Petunia the purple.

The twins now stepped meekly forward and, white and innocent as milk, stood by the font. You couldn't tell them apart. They might have been two identical cherubs cut in stone.

'Let us see,' Mr Candy said to Petunia, 'you are Petunia, with the purple ribbon.'

'No,' Petunia said. 'I'm Zinnia.'

'But you're wearing the purple ribbon.'

'I know. But we changed.'

'Zinnia is supposed to be wearing scarlet. Isn't that right?'

'Yes,' Zinnia said, 'but Petunia hates purple.'

'So Zinnia is now wearing purple and Petunia scarlet?'

'That's right,' they said almost together, 'would you like us to change back again. . . ?'

'Now you are quite sure about this? You wouldn't want me to give you the wrong names, would you?'

'Would it matter?'

'Of course it would matter.'

'Well, I think we changed ribbons three times, but I'm not sure,' Petunia said. 'We had a bit of a tiff. Because I don't like purple.'

'*You* don't like purple—Oh! my Heaven, this is awfully awkward,' Mr Candy said and with fresh desperation turned to Pop. 'Mr Larkin, can you tell me which girl is which? I must be sure.'

'Search me, old man,' Pop said, 'they're more alike some days than others. Ma's the one what knows. You'll have to get Ma.'

'I'll fetch her,' Mariette said.

Still fixing Mr Candy with that dark, celestial stare of hers, Primrose said in a slow soft voice:

'Zinnia has a mole. You'd know if you found that. . . .'

'What's all this?' Ma said.

'We've run into some difficulty, Mrs Larkin,' Mr Candy said. 'Can you please tell me which twin is which. . . ?'

'Nothing for it but to have a look,' she said, seizing the twin she thought was Zinnia by the head and hastily taking her behind the red vestry curtains. . . .

'Sorry, Mr Candy. This is Petunia. I'll warm their bottoms when I get them home.'

The twins, once again indivisible in heavenly, milky innocence, didn't turn a hair and merely waited for the blessing of baptism in patient silence, as if wondering what all the fuss was about.

H.E. BATES (1905—1974)

87. Some twenty-five years ago I knew. . .a fine scholar, an old bachelor, living in a very large rectory. . . . When a labourer desired to have his child privately baptised, he provided a bottle of rum, a pack of cards, a lemon and a basin of pure water, then sent for the parson and the farmer for whom he worked. The religious rite over, the basin was removed, the table cleared, cards and rum produced, and sat down to. On such occasions the rector did not return home till late and the housekeeper left the library window

120

CHRISTENING A BABY

unhasped for the master, but locked the house doors. Under the library window was a violet bed, and it was commonly reported that the rector had on more than one occasion slept in that bed after a christening. Unable to heave up his big body to the sill of the window, he had fallen back among the violets, and there slept off the exertion.

S. BARING GOULD (1832—1924)

Funerals

88.   *July 21, 1821*

Having learnt that Charles Dando of Cridlingcot was killed by a fall from his horse whilst riding from Bristol, I walked to his house to enquire after his family. My anxiety on their account was soon relieved, as I found them sitting round a large table, regaling themselves, without any apparent emotion. Strange it is that the mind should become so callous and indifferent in the midst of the severest trials: their apathy at least, spared me the painful task I had anticipated in my walk to an expected house of mourning, therefore I had no reason to feel distressed on the occasion.

July 24

I was summoned this morning before six o'clock to bury Charles Dando, as the Clerk informed me his corpse had been brought to the Church by his son-in-law and friend, in order to avoid its being arrested, a writ having been sued, and was expected to be executed by persons brought for the purpose. After the grave was dug (for it had not been finished by the Clerk, who expected the funeral at one o'clock) I performed the ceremony, and I must say, with a considerable degree of mental sensation; knowing the whole career of this unfortunate man: the ruin he has entailed on his family; and what is still more dreadful, the dark prospect of retribution in another world. I could not but feel considerably affected, and after the Service was concluded, I addressed the bystanders, begging them to reflect on the serious warning that was held out to all of us to prepare for death; that we might not be taken away unprepared, as was the case of the poor creature we had just committed to the ground. They seemed to be very serious, I cannot but hope it may have its due influence. May it work for good, yet alas! like the moths which flutter round the candle, we see our associates destroyed around us, and madly rush upon the same destruction ourselves.

July 28

I was up early, and commenced writing the sermon I have for some

time been reflecting on, respecting the awful departure of Charles
Dando, on the text 'Let us eat and drink for tomorrow we die. . . .'

July 29
I preached to a crowded audience, so great indeed, the Church
could not contain them. They were for the most part attentive to the
discourse, which spoke of Death and Immortality. I must say, I was
not a little hurt at the total want of all propriety in the people after the
Service was concluded, since instead of returning quietly to their
respective homes in order to reflect on the subject I had taken so
much pains to impress on their minds, and which had so fully
occupied my own, they banished at once all serious reflection by a
merry peal!

JOHN SKINNER (1772—1839)

89.   Yet, surely, when the level ray
       Of some mild eve's declining sun
       Lights on the village pastor, grey
       In years ere ours had well begun—

       As there—in simplest vestment clad,
       He speaks beneath the churchyard tree,
       In solemn tones,—but yet not sad,—
       Of what Man is—what Man shall be!

       And clustering round the grave, half hid
       By that same quiet churchyard yew,
       The rustic mourners bend, to bid
       The dust they loved a last adieu—

RICHARD HARRIS BARHAM (1788—1854)

90.   The grave was twelve feet from the wall. Like all the other
       graves, it lay west and east—the tiny feet would lie towards the
east, awaiting the coming of Christ beyond the sunrise. By one of the

124

trunks of the great elms many wreaths of flowers were laid, piled one on another, each with a card and lines of sympathetic writing; for the baby's death had touched many hearts. A red-haired man stood by them, copying the inscriptions into a penny notebook: he was the village correspondent of the local newspaper, which would describe the flowers as 'a wealth of floral tributes', and for every name included in his list he would probably sell a copy on the following Thursday. . . .

The Rector, in his vestments, walked slowly, with composed face, his hands clasped before him. Behind, the youths bearing the coffin, and the black straggling files of mourners. . . .

Slowly the mourners settled round the grave. The father was a tall man, with a face yellow as tallow, and a black moustache; a thatcher by trade. He swayed, and looked in the grave, with dull, dry eyes. The face of his remaining child, a youth of eighteen, was also sallow, but puffy with weeping. The old grandfather stood beside the grandmother; sometimes he gulped, like the grandson, and stared wildly as the priest recited, in a low and placid voice, the words of the Church of England Burial Service. 'Man that is born of woman hath but a short time to live. . .' the mother, shrunken in black mourning, gave a whimpering cry—'. . . and is full of misery. He cometh up, and is cut down, like a flower; he fleeth as it were a shadow, and never continueth in one stay.'

The parson spoke without feeling. No beauty bloomed in his words, to raise an image in the minds around him. He was sixty years old, and looked forty; perhaps if he had been deeply moved by all the services for burial he had conducted he would have looked eighty. . . .

As the coffin was being lowered, the mother uttered stifled whimpers, while she stared as though penetrating the white composition of the lid, to the small pale face within. She clutched her husband, longing to fling herself down to break the shut lid and to take the little one, whose every laugh and wail and cry in life were still part of her living heart. She heard words, well-worn words, that since childhood had never entered her consciousness: words, 'O Lord God, holy and most merciful Saviour, Lord most holy, O God most

125

mighty, O holy and merciful Saviour.' She tried secretly to smile to herself, and whimpered, 'I believe, I believe;' while her husband held her tightly, his face a duskier yellow. . . .

After the service, the priest turned to the mother and said, in a voice more like his own, 'Do not grieve, Mrs Ridd. She is now safe in the arms of Jesus, and one day you will see her there.' 'Aiy, aiy!' said the old fisherman, the baby's grandfather. 'She'm safe i' th' arms of Jesus,' and looked at the sky. He walked away, to get a glass of beer, and looked into the sun's face, which dried his tears, and gave strength of life after grief.

HENRY WILLIAMSON (1895—1977)

126

127

Pluralities

91.   I had gathered from my respectable friend . . . that Morning
      Service commenced at Compton Martin at eleven o'clock, so I
started fully resolved to say my prayers on Sunday, February 9th, in
this favoured part of Somersetshire if I possibly could. . . .

I started a quarter before eight on Sunday morning. . . . There
stood the church full in front of me on the side of the hill and the
Gothic parsonage peeping out from amongst the leafless trees, but
no sound of Sabbath-going bells reached. 'Can you tell me, my
excellent friend,' said I to a good-looking farmer who passed me, 'the
hour of Service at Compton Martin?'

'It was half-past nine *this* morning, Sir,' said he, 'as Mr Brown had
to go over and do duty at (I think he said) Nempnett.'

'Then I have had my ride for nothing,' said I, 'for it is now half-past
ten. Service was at eleven o'clock last Sunday; pray how do the
parishioners become acquainted with these changes, if Prayers shift
from one hour to the other in this way?'

'He sends round the clerk to our houses on Saturday or some
other day during the week.'

'Well,' thought I, as I paused in doubt as to what I should do. . . .

My friend seeing my indecision said, 'If you turn back you will be in
time for Prayers at Chew-Stoke, Sir.' I thanked him for the advice
and turned back, and soon heard old Bilby's beautiful bells pealing
out from Chew tower. . . .

As I entered the church yard the bell ceased. Not to be late, I hur-
ried towards the south porch and—*met the congregation coming
out!* Bless my soul, thought I, here's another disappointment! 'Are
prayers over my good lad?' said I to the first of a school of boys in blue
coats, breeches and black stockings and bands. 'No Sir,' replied the
lad, 'there are none today; the parson's taken very bad.'

JOSEPH LEECH (1815—1893)

92.   One parson came and people said,
      'Alas! Our former Vicar's dead!

128

And this new man is far more "Low"
Than dear old Reverend so-and-so,
And far too earnest in his preaching,
We do not really like his teaching,
He seems to think we're simply fools
Who've never been to Sunday Schools.'
That Vicar left, and by and by
A new one came, 'He's much too "High",'
The people said, 'too like a saint,
His incense makes our Mavis faint.'
So now he's left and they're alone
Without a Vicar of their own.
The living's been amalgamated
With one next door they've always hated.

JOHN BETJEMAN (1908—1984)

93.　Nick chose to attend a mid-morning Parish Communion service in Sparham, a village of just over 1,000 inhabitants. . . . By 10 o'clock there were 23 people in church. . . . As the clock struck 10, Nick was beginning to wonder why he had seen no signs of the vicar. Then, suddenly, the church door burst open and the vicar came rushing in. . . and flew round the church putting things out. The problem is that the vicar of Sparham has two other churches in his care and that morning he had already celebrated Communion in them both, at 8.00 a.m. and 9.00 a.m.

Before the vicar had arrived, Nick had felt that there was an atmosphere of quiet prayer in the church, an appropriate preparation for worship. All this was rudely destroyed as the vicar tried to organise himself for the service. Nick felt sorry for the congregation; he felt even sorrier for the parish priest who had allowed himself to get pushed into such a tight schedule. Nick began to wonder whether it really was helpful for a parish priest to celebrate Communion at 8.00 a.m., 9.00 a.m. and 10.00 a.m. in three different churches, and, if this was inevitable, whether it would be possible to encourage greater lay participation in preparing the churches before the priest arrived.

129

The service began just seven minutes late. The vicar set off at a breathless pace, and none of the congregation could keep up. Consequently, the congregation took very little active part in the service and only joined in the prayers with a half-hearted mumble. They seemed to have become accustomed to being treated as spectators rather than as participants and so no longer really tried to participate. The brisk pace of the service meant that it was all over in forty-eight minutes. . . .

There was no choir to help lead the singing, and the vicar felt that it was his responsibility to give a loud lead. In fact, he paid little attention to the speed of the organ or indeed to the words in the hymn book. The congregation preferred to listen to this battle between the organist and the vicar, without themselves taking sides. . . .

After the service, the vicar stood by the door as the congregation went out and he tried to speak to each one of them. . . . When it came to Nick's turn, the vicar shook him by the hand and said that he would be always welcome to come again. Nick replied that he was just passing though. The vicar was not listening. 'No matter; you'll always be welcome,' he repeated. Nick agreed that it didn't really seem to matter at all.

LESLIE J. FRANCIS (1947 –   )

94.   I march'd three miles through scorching sand,
With zeal in heart, and notes in hand;
I rode four more to Great St Mary,
Using four legs, when two were weary:
To three fair virgins I did tie men,
In the close bonds of pleasing Hymen;
I dipp'd two babes in holy water,
And purified their mother after.
Within an hour and eke a half,
I preach'd three congregations deaf;
Where, thundering out, with lungs long winded,
I chopp'd so fast, that few there minded.
My emblem, the laborious sun,

Saw all these mighty labours done
Before one race of his was run.
All this perform'd by Robert Hewit:
What mortal else could e'er go through it!

JONATHAN SWIFT (1667—1745)

ABOUT THE PARISH

4. ABOUT THE PARISH

Visiting

95.   The Rector visited each cottage in turn, working his way conscientiously round the hamlet from door to door, so that by the
end of the year he had called upon everybody. When he tapped with
his gold-headed cane at a cottage door there would come a sound of
scuffling within, as unseemly objects were hustled out of sight, for
the whisper would have gone round that he had been seen getting
over the stile and his knock would have been recognized.

The women received him with respectful tolerance. A chair was
dusted with an apron and the doing of housework or cooking was
suspended while his hostess, seated uncomfortably on the edge of
one of her own chairs, waited for him to open the conversation.
When the weather had been discussed, the health of the inmates
and absent children inquired about, and the progress of the pig and
the prospect of the allotment crops, there came an awkward pause,
during which both racked their brains to find something to talk
about. There was nothing. The Rector never mentioned religion.
That was looked upon in the parish as one of his chief virtues, but it
limited the possible topics of conversation. Apart from his autocratic
ideas, he was a kindly man, and he had come to pay a friendly call,
hoping, no doubt, to get to know and to understand his parishioners
better. But the gulf between them was too wide; neither he nor his
hostess could bridge it. The kindly inquiries made and answered,
they had nothing more to say to each other, and, after much 'ah-ing'

and 'er-ing', he would rise from his seat, and be shown out with alac-
rity.

FLORA THOMPSON (1876—1947)

96. *Monday, 7 June*

I walked to Langley Grove through the mowing grass. Dear little Katie opened the door to me and her father Farmer Lessiter was better and sitting downstairs at tea. When I went away and shook hands with him at parting he gave me a kind look out of his blue eyes and said, 'I wish I were as strong as you, Sir. I know you must be a very strong man. When I was in bed the other day and you shook hands with me I felt as if an electrifying machine had gone all through me and I feel the same now. I made the remark after you were gone that you must be a very strong man. There is something so stiff to lean against in your grasp.'

'Oh,' I said, 'you will be as strong as I am again in a few days.'

'No,' said the stout farmer, with a sad shake of the head and a sorrowful look in his blue eyes. 'No, I shall never be as strong as you are any more.'

Tuesday, 8 June

How delightful it is in these sweet summer evenings to wander from cottage to cottage and from farm to farm exchanging bright words and looks with the beautiful girls at their garden gates and talking to the kindly people sitting at their cottage doors or meeting in the lane when their work is done. How sweet it is to pass from house to house welcome and beloved everywhere by young and old, to meet the happy loving smiles of the dear children at their evening play in the lanes and fields and to meet with no harsher reproach than this, 'It is a longful while since you have been to see us. We do all love to see you coming and we do miss you sorely when you are away.'

Saturday, 12 June

I went to see my dear little lover Mary Tavener, the deaf and half dumb child. When I opened the door of the poor old crazy cottage in

134

the yard the girl uttered a passionate inarticulate cry of joy and running to me she flung her arms round my neck and covered me with kisses. Well, I have lived and I have been loved, and no one can take this from me.

Monday, 14 June
Villaging. Visited Mrs Lawrence who amused me by a description of how she fell down the cellar stairs from top to bottom by reason of her 'grasping on vacancy' instead of grasping a pound of candles which were hanging against the wall. When she revived herself and came up, 'Charles,' she said to her husband, 'I am almost dead. I have fallen from the top of the cellar stairs to the bottom.' 'You couldn't have done it,' said Charles incredulously from under the bedclothes. 'I have done it, Charles,' she shouted, infuriated at his unbelief.

Tuesday, 22 June
I have been working all the afternoon in our meadows with the haymakers, Farmer Jacob Knight, John Couzens, Hannah, Mary and Joseph Hatherell and Emma Halliday. We have got a lot of beautiful green fragrant hay up in cock.

FRANCIS KILVERT (1840—1872)

97.　Parsons old and parsons new would proceed often from their churches, vicarages and rectories to talk to my mother, who adored parsons. Les and I did not—especially one who always came at tea-time, had several cups of tea on the cheap and always stood with upped frock-coat tails in front of our fire.

He came one afternoon when we were about to have tea and we wanted to get the meal over quickly because we were going out rabbiting.

'Now, Leslie! Who remembahs last Sunday's text?'

Not Leslie! The parson turned to Mother. 'Well, Mrs Mays. What did you think of my sermon, eh? Do you think that I am now finding the hearts of my flock?' and so on.

135

'Come now, Leslie, do have a try!'

Leslie had a try, a poor one.

'No, no, no, Leslie! ... "To do MY duty in THAT state of life unto which it shall please God to call me." That is how it goes, Leslie! Not "THAT" duty in "MY" state of life. Oh, deah me NO!'

At this point there came an almighty bang; smoke swirled, fire flew and the parson ran yelping down our back garden as though the Devil had him by the coat tails.

Somewhat disobliged because our rabbiting was being held up, Leslie had slipped into the fire a 12-bore Ely cartridge loaded with No.4 pigeon shot.

SPIKE MAYS (1907—   )

Hospitality

98.   Another and very frequent visitor to Nightmare Abbey, was
       the Reverend Mr Larynx, the vicar of Claydyke, a village about
ten miles distant;—a good natured accommodating divine, who was
always most obligingly ready to take dinner and a bed at the house of
any country gentleman in distress for a companion. Nothing came
amiss to him,—a game at billiards, at chess, at draughts, at
backgammon, at piquet, or at all-fours in a *tête-a-tête*, or any game
on the cards, round, square, or triangular, in a party of any number
exceeding two. He would even dance among friends, rather than
that a lady, even if she were on the wrong side of thirty, should sit still
for want of a partner. For a ride, a walk, or a sail, in the morning,—a
song after dinner, a ghost story after supper,—a bottle of port with
the squire, or a cup of green tea with his lady,—for all or any of these,
or for anything else that was agreeable to anyone else, consistently
with the dye of his coat, the Reverend Mr Larynx was at all times
equally ready.

THOMAS LOVE PEACOCK (1785—1866)

99.   The new passon cum on Saterday; a young lad of 20 yeres or
       so. I be glad we did do much cookeing for he did ett much,
being clemmed of his journie. We to church on the Sabboth, and did
heare a plessent sermon. John did nod as alwayes, but the passon
did pleese me much, for ye did not tell us that the divvel would hav us
for caring for sum monies, but did say the world be a verrie good
plase to live in; and be good to the poore, was the true religun. To
which I do hartilie agree.

Then we home to dinner, carrying off Mistress Prue ande her sister
Livvie; where we did find Sarah had put all reddie. We did have roste
goose stuffed with boiled egges and sweete appels, which did cum
out nice and jouisey; sum shepe mutton, and 2 roste hens; a round of
befe boiled, and taties and soe on—as well as a mylke pudden, and a
appel and divers others. To which all did do justis, and Mistress Prue
praising Sarahs cookeing much, did pleese me. And I did see passon

look at Sarah verrie prettie. After dinner John and passon out to see
sum of the village folke, to see how they do; which be verrie nice of
him, being the firste passon I ever knowed to do so.

ANNE HUGHES (18th century)

100. Our party, on the fifth of November, passed off very well. . . .
The Reverend Michael Millward was mighty in important
dogmas and sententious jokes, pompous anecdotes, and oracular
discourses, dealt out for the edification of the whole assembly in
general, and of the admiring Mrs Markham, the polite Mr Lawrence,
the sedate Mary Millward, the quiet Richard Wilson, and the matter
of fact Robert, in particular,—as being the most attentive
llisteners. . . .
'I don't take wine, Mrs Markham,' said Mr Millward, upon the
introduction of that beverage; 'I'll take a little of your home-brewed
ale. I always prefer your home-brewed to anything else.'
Flattered at this compliment, my mother rang the bell, and a china
jug of our best ale was presently brought, and set before the worthy
gentleman who so well knew how to appreciate its excellencies.
'Now THIS is the thing!' cried he, pouring out a glass of the same in a
long stream, skilfully directed from the jug to the tumbler, so as to
produce much foam without spilling a drop; and having surveyed it
for a moment opposite the candle, he took a deep draught, and then
smacked his lips, drew a long breath, and refilled his glass, my
mother looking on with the greatest satisfaction.
'There's nothing like this, Mrs Markham!' said he; 'I always
maintain that there's nothing to compare with your home-brewed
ale.'
'I'm sure I'm glad you like it, sir. I always look after the brewing
myself, as well as the cheese and the butter—I like to have things well
done, while we're about it.'
'Quite right, Mrs Markham!'
'But then, Mr Millward, you don't think it wrong to take a little wine
now and then—or a little spirits either?' said my mother, as she
handed a smoking tumbler of gin and water to Mrs Wilson, who

138

affirmed that wine sat heavy on her stomach, and whose son Robert was at that moment helping himself to a pretty stiff glass of the same.

'By no means!' replied the oracle, with a Jove-like nod; 'these things are all blessings and mercies, if we only know how to make use of them.'

ANNE BRONTË (1820—1849)

101.   When I returned to the drawing-room, I found the company seated round the fire, listening to the parson, who was deeply ensconced in a high-backed oaken chair, the work of some cunning artificer of yore, which had been brought from the library for his particular accommodation. From this venerable piece of furniture, with which his shadowy figure and dark weazen face so admirably accorded, he was dealing forth strange accounts of the popular superstitions and legends of the surrounding country, with which he had become acquainted in the course of his antiquarian researches. I am half inclined to think that the old gentleman was himself somewhat tinctured with superstition, as men are very apt to be who live a recluse and studious life in a sequestered part of the country, and pore over black-letter tracts, so often filled with the marvellous and supernatural. He gave us several anecdotes of the fancies of the neighbouring peasantry, concerning the effigy of the crusader which lay on the tomb by the church altar. As it was the only monument of the kind in that part of the country, it had always been regarded with feelings of superstition by the goodwives of the village. It was said to get up from the tomb and walk the rounds of the churchyard in stormy nights, particularly when it thundered; and one old woman, whose cottage bordered on the churchyard, had seen it, through the windows of the church, when the moon shone, slowly pacing up and down the aisles. It was the belief that some wrong had been left unredressed by the deceased, or some treasure hidden, which kept the spirit in a state of trouble and restlessness. Some talked of gold and jewels buried in the tomb, over which the spectre kept watch; and there was a story current of a sexton in old times who endeavoured to break his way to the coffin at night; but

139

just as he reached it, received a violent blow from the marble hand of the effigy, which stretched him senseless on the pavement. These tales were often laughed at by some of the sturdier among the rustics, yet when night came on, there were many of the stoutest unbelievers that were shy of venturing alone in the footpath that led across the churchyard.

WASHINGTON IRVING (1783—1859)

Social Concern

102.   In visiting the labouring families of my parish, as my duty led me, I could not but observe with concern their mean and distressed condition. I found them in general but indifferently fed; badly clothed; some children without shoes and stockings; very few put to school; and most families in debt to little shopkeepers. In short, there was scarcely any appearance of comfort about their dwellings, except that the children looked tolerably healthy. Yet I could not impute the wretchedness I saw either to sloth or wastefulness. For I knew that the farmers were careful that the men should not want employment; and had they been given to drinking, I am sure I should have heard enough of it. And I commonly found the women, when not working in the fields, well occupied at home; seldom indeed earning money; but baking their bread, washing and mending their garments, and rocking the cradle.

These poor people, in assigning the cause of their misery, agreed in ascribing it to the high prices of the necessaries of life. 'Every thing (said they) is so dear, that we can hardly live.' In order to assure myself, whether this was really the case, I enquired into the particulars of their earnings and expenses; and wrote the same down at the time, just as I received them from each family respectively, guarding as well as I could against error and deception. The . . . accounts are the result of that enquiry, and they shew that the cause assigned is founded in fact.

These accounts of the earnings and expenses of labouring families, in my own parish were collected about Easter 1787, when affairs relating to the poor were under the consideration of the Parliament and the public. From what loose information I could then gather near home, I saw sufficient reason to believe, that they presented but too faithful a view of the general distress of such families throughout this and the neighbouring counties. And the vast increase of the poor-rate, at that time every where a subject of complaint, rendered it very probable that the same misery had overspread the kingdom.

On my suggesting this to some friends who interest themselves in the welfare of the poor, we thought this matter deserving of a fuller scrutiny. And in order to collect information, an abstract of these accounts was printed, and many copies were distributed. We supposed that two or three papers returned from every county, carefully filled up, would furnish us amply with the information we desired. I have to regret that a greater number of those distributed papers has not been returned. The few I have received confirm the opinion previously entertained of the general distress of labouring people, and of the insufficiency of their wages for the supply of their wants.

DAVID DAVIES (1745—1819)

103.   The Rev. Sydney Godolphin Osborne won a national reputation as an unpaid contributor to *The Times*. His letters were always controversial, if not by their content then by their provocative and even vitriolic form. His strong sense of his own social position and personal identity ensured that he had no inhibitions about using the most ferocious language. His early interest in medicine became intensified as a result of his observation of the generally unsanitary conditions throughout the country and the periodical epidemics of typhus and cholera. His heart would sink when he did his cottage rounds during a cholera visitation, and in 1853 he described the disease sardonically as 'the great scavenger of our race'. 'The cholera is cleaning out our human cesspools, removing sewage—mortal and immortal,' he noted grimly.

He began a series of careful experiments in the rectory on the causes of cholera, and finally decided that germs were responsible. In 1854 he described in print how he had trapped organic material in the effluvia of a cesspool by dropping a metal pipe into it to act as an air shaft and then examining the air under the microscope. He found 'countless masses of animated, active bodies' and felt sure that some were a new genus which could also be found where vegetable and animal matter decayed. As a good Christian he was convinced that all those bodies had their allotted place in the balance of nature and were nature's cleansing agents. In his usual

142

bluff manner he wrote that 'if the public could be brought to *see* that which floats in what they *smell* from sewers and cesspools, they would be more careful in the removal of filth in such a way as to, as far as may be, limit the escape of its life-crowded atmosphere.' In thus hinting at a germ theory Osborne was far ahead of his time, for the theory did not gain general credence until T.H. Huxley came out in favour of it after 1870.

BRENDA COLLOMS (1919—   )

104. *Wednesday February 5 1800*

Went up to Mr Amen in the quarry. Found him with two savage kind of men, Old Ware and his son. They were both full of complaints against one Davies who came from Stowey to this parish and has now informed against several persons for cutting Lord Egmont's wood. This Davies is the greatest scoundrel and rascal, pilferer and wood-cutter that comes into any parish. I smiled at their complaints and said 'Well lads you have nothing to do but look sharp and I'll warrant you he may be caught at the same tricks then show the scoundrel no mercy but haul him to the Justice at once.' They vowed to watch him narrowly, nothing like setting a thief to catch a thief.

Tuesday February 25

Old Scoundrel Ware and his son passed by. It is said they are going to burn the greater scoundrel Davies in effigy for informing against them for cutting wood, Lord Egmont's wood. Sing Tantararara Rogues All. Went to Asholt and married a couple, the lady did not appear very small about the waist. Saw a large party go up the Hill to burn Davies in effigy. They paraded first through Stowey and the Scoundrel Davies had the impudence to march before them all the time.

Monday March 24

The horse seems much better, and we shall, I believe bring him round. Weymouth's children have committed great depredations

143

.on my new hedges by drawing off the laid sticks. There is wood sufficient on the hills and yet these wretches prefer damaging the hedges
of their neighbours to fetching it. I must call them to account for this.

WILLIAM HOLLAND (1746—1819)

Sickness

105.   One day in the year 1694 (I have good reason to remember
        it), Doctor Tusher ran into Castlewood House, with a face of
consternation, saying that the malady had made its appearance at
the blacksmith's house in the village, and that one of the maids there
was down in smallpox. . . .

Little Lady Beatrix screamed out at Doctor Tusher's news; and my
lord cried out, 'God bless me!' He was a brave man, and not afraid of
death in any shape but this. He was very proud of his pink
complexion and fair hair—but the idea of death by smallpox scared
him beyond all other ends. 'We will take the children and ride away
to-morrow to Walcote:'this was my lord's small house, inherited
from his mother, near to Winchester.

'That is the best refuge in case the disease spreads,' said Doctor
Tusher. ' 'Tis awful to think of it beginning at the ale-house; half the
people of the village have visited that to-day, or the blacksmith's
which is the same thing. My clerk Nahum lodges with them—I can
never go into my reading-desk and have that fellow so near me. I
won't have that man near me.'

'If a parishioner dying in the small pox sent to you, would you not
go?'asked my lady, looking up from her frame of work, with her calm
blue eyes.

'By the Lord, I wouldn't,' said my lord.

'We are not in a Popish country; and a sick man doth not absolutely need absolution and confession,' said the Doctor. ' 'Tis true
they are a comfort and a help to him when attainable, and to be
administered with hope of good. But in a case where the life of a parish priest in the midst of his flock is highly valuable to them, he is not
called upon to risk it (and therewith the lives, future prospects, and
temporal, even spiritual welfare of his own family) for the sake of a
single person, who is not very likely in a condition even to understand the religious message whereof the priest is the bringer—being
uneducated, and likewise stupefied or delirious by disease. If your
ladyship or his lordship, my excellent good friend and patron, were
to take it —'

'God forbid!' cried my lord.

'Amen,' continued Doctor Tusher. 'Amen to that prayer, my very good lord! for your sake I would lay my life down'— and, to judge from the alarmed look of the Doctor's purple face, you would have thought that that sacrifice was about to be called for instantly.'

WILLIAM MAKEPEACE THACKERAY (1811—1867)

106.　Mr Richardson, an excise man near Buxton, a serious young man, was seized with ye small pox. When I came to him I prescribed a womit which succeeded well. Ye small pox appeared on ye 4th day of ye confluent kind and very malignant with many purple spots intermixed. On the 12th day ye 2nd feavar was very high and on ye following days he was delirious. I prescribed opiates and alexipharmicks and 2 episparick plaisters. Through God's assistance he recovered.

JAMES CLEGG (1679—1755)

107.　And he was kind, and loved to sit
In the low hut or garnished cottage,
And praise the farmer's homely wit,
And share the widow's homelier pottage:
At his approach complaint grew mild;
And when his hand unbarred the shutter,
The clammy lips of fever smiled
The welcome which they could not utter.

WINTHROP MACKWORTH PRAED (1802—1839)

108.　He ceases now the feeble help to crave
Of man; and silent sinks into the grave.
But ere his death some pious doubts arise,
Some simple fears, which 'bold bad' men despise;
Fain would he ask the parish-priest to prove
His title certain to the joys above:

For this he sends the murmuring nurse, who calls
The holy stranger to these dismal walls:
And doth not he, the pious man, appear,
He, 'passing rich with forty pounds a year?'
Ah! no; a shepherd of a different stock,
And far unlike him, feeds this little flock:
A jovial youth, who thinks his Sunday's task
As much as God or man can fairly ask;
The rest he gives to loves and labours light,
To fields the morning, and to feasts the night;
None better skill'd the noisy pack to guide,
To urge their chase, to cheer them or to chide;
A sportsman keen, he shoots through half the day,
And, skill'd at whist, devotes the night to play:
Then, while such honours bloom around his head,
Shall he sit sadly by the sick man's bed,
To raise the hope he feels not, or with zeal
To combat fears that e'en the pious feel?

GEORGE CRABBE (1754—1832)

109.   I see him trudging through muddy lanes and over long
sweeps of plover-haunted pastures to visit a cottager's dying
wife. He takes her meat and wine from his own table, and that not a
little only but liberally. According to his lights also, he administers
what he is pleased to call spiritual consolation.

'I am afraid I'm going to Hell, Sir,' says the sick woman with a
whine. 'Oh, Sir, save me, save me, don't let me go there. I couldn't
stand it, Sir, I should die with fear, the very thought of it drives me into
a cold sweat all over.'

'Mrs Thompson,' says Theobald gravely, 'you must have faith in
the precious blood of your Redeemer; it is He alone who can save
you.'

'But are you sure, Sir,' says she, looking wistfully at him, 'that He
will forgive me—for I've not been a very good woman, indeed I
haven't—and if God would only say "Yes" outright with His mouth
when I ask whether my sins are forgiven me —'

147

'But they *are* forgiven you, Mrs Thompson,' says Theobald with some sternness, for the same ground has been gone over a good many times already, and he has borne the unhappy woman's misgivings now for a full quarter of an hour. Then he puts a stop to the conversation by repeating prayers taken from the 'Visitation of the Sick' and overawes the poor wretch from expressing further anxiety as to her condition.

'Can't you tell me, Sir,' she exclaims piteously, as she sees that he is preparing to go away, 'can't you tell me that there is no Day of Judgement, and that there is no such place as Hell? I can do without the Heaven, Sir, but I cannot do with the Hell.' Theobald is much shockèd.

'Mrs Thompson,' he rejoins impressively, 'let me implore you to suffer no doubt concerning these two corner-stones of our religion to cross your mind at a moment like the present. If there is one thing more certain than another it is that we shall all appear before the Judgement Seat of Christ, and that the wicked will be consumed in a lake of everlasting fire. Doubt this, Mrs Thompson, and you are lost.'

The poor woman buries her fevered head in the coverlet in a paroxysm of fear which at last finds relief in tears.

'Mrs Thompson,' says Theobald, with his hand on the door, 'compose yourself, be calm; you must please to take my word for it that at the Day of Judgement your sins will be all washed white in the blood of the Lamb, Mrs Thompson. Yes,' he exclaims frantically, 'though they be as scarlet, yet shall they be as white as wool,' and he makes off as fast as he can from the fetid atmosphere of the cottage to the pure air outside. Oh, how thankful he is when the interview is over. . . .

He has left meat and wine—that he can do; he will call again and will leave more meat and wine; day after day he trudges over the same plover-haunted fields, and listens at the end of his walk to the same agony of forebodings, which day after day he silences, but does not remove, till at last a merciful weakness renders the sufferer careless of her future, and Theobald is satisfied that her mind is now peacefully at rest in Jesus.

Samuel Butler (1835—1902)

148

110.   I had a call from a very worried lady whose husband had, for
        several years, been acting in a strange way from time to time.
He would be quite normal for a few weeks then suddenly it was as if
his whole personality became transformed into an aggressive,
domineering and at times enraged character. He had sought
psychiatric help without any results. His wife summed up the
problem by saying that she had had fourteen years of married hell. I
agreed to see the husband, so with a friend to drive, they set off on
the seventy-mile journey to North Molton at nine o'clock in the
evening, and arrived at my vicarage just before midnight. The man
was by this time in a very disturbed state, and he rushed through the
door shouting, 'Where is Fred Pennington? I want to get hold of
him.' I was by this time quite prepared for anything he might do or
say, having spent the previous two hours in prayer and meditation.
Dorothy took the wife and friend into the kitchen and gave them
coffee, while I began what was to be the first of many fascinating and
dramatic cases in my ministry to the possessed.

While watching my colleague at work previously I had realised
that the most important part of my exorcism was to make a correct
diagnosis. I knew how subtle evil personified could be, and how it
could cause a person to act and say things that were completely
false. I knew, too, that when under hypnosis a person always
answered truthfully to any question, so I decided to use that medium
as my method of diagnosis. Having put the man into that state, I
proceeded to question him until I was fully convinced that here was
a genuine case of possession.

I felt I was being guided to do two things in this my first case of
exorcism. First, to carry out that exorcism while the man was still
under hypnosis, and in so doing to by-pass, as it were, his conscious
mind, and simply be a channel for Christ in his work of destroying the
evil power which was controlling this man. Secondly, to know myself
to be surrounded by Christ's protecting power, so that I lost all sense
of fear, and simply allowed Christ to take my lips and speak through
them whatever words He desired. This is how I have acted in every
exorcism since that day.

The manifestations of that first exorcism could not have been more dramatic if they had come from some novelist's pen. As I made the sign of the cross, while commanding evil to depart in Christ's name, the man suddenly opened his eyes. This is unknown in an ordinary session of hypnotherapy, but they had become blood red, and twice their normal size. They became fixed on me, and at the same time his lips seemed to twist into a leering sneer so that his teeth appeared as fangs. He then arose from his chair, still under hypnosis of course, and came towards me with his hands outstretched as if they were claws. As he slowly approached me, he began to speak in a voice that was totally unlike his own. He said, 'I am not coming out of him. I don't want to come out of him.'He repeated these words several times, getting closer and closer to me until his hands were almost touching my face. I stood quite still and continued to use the form of exorcism with which I had begun; suddenly and without any warning, he collapsed on the floor where I noticed he was frothing at the mouth.

I felt instinctively that I had to kneel beside him and lay my hands on his head in healing prayer, and at the same time I sought to heal any memories of his traumatic experience in his unconscious mind which might otherwise later become part of his conscious state, and so cause trouble there. I then told him to sit in his chair where I woke him from his hypnotic trance. We afterwards went for a walk and I found him to be a completely changed man.

F. PENNINGTON (1911—   )

Death

111. I wrote to Mr Etheridge of Simpson, Brother-in-Law to
      Farmer Turn, who died at West Blecheley yesterday of the
small pox, to let him be put into the grave this evening, and I would
read the Burial Service over him to-morrow; as hardly any of the
parish had had the distemper and few of the clergy could be got to
bury him; as even those who had had it themselves, were afraid of
carrying the infection to their wives and children. He readily
assented to my proposal; Mrs Willis so alarmed, that she went out of
the parish for a week or two.

WILLIAM COLE (1714—1782)

112. The vicar called at Holland Farm, and, waiting for Stephen to
      come in from the fields, sat with the children in the garden.
'You must miss your mother very much.'
'Of course,' said Chris, in a curt tone. 'She happens to be dead.'
The vicar was shocked. He himself never spoke of death. He felt
he had a duty to the four children facing him.
'Don't you know where your mother is?' he asked, eyeing each of
them in turn. 'Surely now, you can tell me that?'
Chris and Joanna looked away. The vicar's question embarrassed
them. They knew what he wanted them to say, but they had no use
for the life hereafter, even it its existence could be proved. He turned
his gaze on Jamesy instead.
'What about you, young man? Can you tell me where your mother
is?'
'Yes,' said Jamesy, 'she's in her grave.'
When Stephen came, the vicar stood up. He would not stay more
than a moment, he said. He knew how busy farmers were.
'I came to see if I could help. With a young family like yours, I know
what problems there must be, and if there's anything I or my wife can
do—'
'You're very kind,' Stephen said, 'But my cousin, Miss Skeine, is

151

coming back from India soon. She's going to make her home here,
and look after us all, my children and me.'

'So glad, so glad,' the vicar said.

MARY E. PEARCE (1932—   )

113.   Now once again the gloomy scene explore,
Less gloomy now; the bitter hour is o'er,
The man of many sorrows sighs no more.—
Up yonder hill, behold how sadly slow
The bier moves winding from the vale below;
There lie the happy dead, from trouble free,
And the glad parish pays the frugal fee:
No more, O Death! thy victim starts to hear
Churchwarden stern, or kingly overseer;
No more the farmer claims his humble bow,
Thou art his lord, the best of tyrants thou!
Now to the church behold the mourners come,
Sedately torpid and devoutly dumb;
The village children now their games suspend,
To see the bier that bears their ancient friend;
For he was one in all their idle sport,
And like a monarch ruled their little court.
The pliant bow he form'd, the flying ball,
The bat, the wicket, were his labours all;
Him now they follow to his grave, and stand
Silent and sad, and gazing, hand in hand;
While bending low, their eager eyes explore
The mingled relics of the parish poor:
The bell tolls late, the moping owl flies round,
Fear marks the flight and magnifies the sound;
The busy priest, detain'd by weightier care,
Defers his duty till the day of prayer;
And, waiting long, the crowd retire distress'd,
To think a poor man's bones should lie unbless'd.

GEORGE CRABBE (1754—1832)

152

114.　But the hour came, at last, that ended Mr Earnshaw's troubles on earth. He died quietly in his chair one October evening, seated by the fire-side. A high wind blustered round the house, and roared in the chimney: it sounded wild and stormy. . . . Joseph told me to put on my cloak and run to Gimmerton for the doctor and the parson. I could not guess the use that either would be of, then. However, I went, through wind and rain, and brought one, the doctor, back with me; the other said he would come in the morning. Leaving Joseph to explain matters, I ran to the children's room: the door was ajar, I saw they had never lain down, though it was past midnight; but they were calmer, and did not need me to console them. The little souls were comforting each other with better thoughts than I could have hit on: no parson in the world ever pictured heaven so beautifully as they did.

EMILY BRONTË (1818—1848)

115.　Those villagers who since the War had bought their own cottages, and the farmers' wives and daughters, thought that the new marble stones, with their immaculate letterings, and the artificial flower wreaths made of marble-chip waste from the stone-mason's yards, 'very nice' and 'lovely'. Perhaps the appearance of the wire-caged 'everlasting' marble flowers on the graves of their dead made them feel superior in the eyes of the other church-goers walking in their best clothes through the lych-gate on Sunday morning. It is doubtful if the human mind would connect the glass domes and wire-cages with the dead; and yet, when the Rector wrote in his parochial letter in the *Monthly Bulletin* that the 'lobster pots and bird cages' on the graves were unsightly, there was much indignation because he had spoken thus about the sacredness of the dead. One man named Matthew Hammett was very upset by the comment; his mother had recently died, and he had ordered an extra large marble bouquet at twenty-five shillings.

It was not long, however, before the churchyard was void of marble flowers. Tulips, wallflowers, pansies, bell-flowers, aubretia, and other flowering plants grew in their places. Where once nettles

153

and docks grew under the western elms, over the unmarked
mounds of the suicides and nameless drowned sailors, daffodils and
primroses flowered in spring, appraised by the village.

The Church Council approved the scale of charges laid down by
the Rector for burials. Mr Crib the sexton got five shillings for digging
a grave; the Rector, who after all had to live, got two hundred shillings for the use of his words and gestures, the modern varnished,
rubber-tyred, ball-bearing coffin-carrier, and the soil.

HENRY WILLIAMSON (1895—1977)

Squires

116.   The very next village is famous for the differences and con-
tentions that rise between the parson and the squire, who live
in a perpetual state of war. The parson is always at the squire, and the
squire, to be revenged on the parson, never comes to church. The
squire has made all his tenants atheists and tithe-stealers; while the
parson instructs them every Sunday in the dignity of his order, and
insinuates to them, almost in every sermon, that he is a better man
than his patron. In short, matters have come to such an extremity,
that the squire has not said his prayers either in public or private this
half-year; and that the parson threatens him, if he does not mend his
manner, to pray for him in the face of the whole congregation.

Feuds of this nature, though too frequent in the country, are very
fatal to the ordinary people; who are so used to be dazzled with
riches, that they pay as much deference to the understanding of a
man of an estate, as of a man of learning; and are very hardly brought
to regard any truth, how important soever it may be, that is preached
to them, when they know there are several men of five hundred a
year who do not believe it.

JOSEPH ADDISON (1672—1719)

117.   In many places there is still a greater man belonging to the
church, than either the parson or the clerk himself. The
person I mean is the Squire; who, like the King, may be styled Head
of the Church in his own parish. If the benefice be in his own gift, the
vicar is his creature, and of consequence entirely at his devotion; or,
if the care of the church be left to a curate, the Sunday fees of roast
beef and plum pudding, and a liberty to shoot in the manor, will bring
him as much under the Squire's command as his dogs and horses.
For this reason the bell is often kept tolling and the people waiting in
the churchyard an hour longer than the usual time; nor must the
service begin until the Squire has strutted up the aisle, and seated
himself in the great pew in the chancel. The length of the sermon is
also measured by the will of the Squire, as formerly by the hour-

glass: and I know one parish where the preacher has always the complaisance to conclude his discourse, however abruptly, the minute that the Squire gives the signal, by rising up after his nap.

WILLIAM COWPER (1731—1800)

118.   A few privileged villagers, who were allowed to be spectators on these great occasions, were seated on benches placed for them near the door; and great was the admiration and satisfaction in that quarter when the couples had formed themselves for the dance, and the Squire led off with Mrs Crackenthorp, joining hands with the Rector and Mrs Osgood. That was as it should be—that was what everybody had been used to—and the charter of Raveloe seemed to be renewed by the ceremony. It was not thought of as an unbecoming levity for the old and middle-aged people to dance a little before sitting down to cards, but rather as part of their social duties. For what were these if not to be merry at appropriate times, interchanging visits and poultry with due frequency, paying each other old-established compliments in sound traditional phrases, passing well-tried personal jokes, urging your guests to eat and drink too much out of hospitality, and eating and drinking too much in your neighbour's house to show that you liked your cheer? And the parson naturally set an example in these social duties. For it would not have been possible for the Raveloe mind, without a peculiar revelation, to know that a clergyman should be a pale-faced memento of solemnities, instead of a reasonably faulty man whose exclusive authority to read prayers and preach, to christen, marry, and bury you, necessarily co-existed with the right to sell you the ground to be buried in and to take tithe in kind; on which last point, of course, there was a little grumbling, but not to the extent of irreligion. . . .

There was no reason, then, why the Rector's dancing should not be received as part of the fitness of things quite as much as the Squire's, or why, on the other hand, Mr Macey's official respect should restrain him from subjecting the parson's performance to that criticism with which minds of extraordinary acuteness must necessarily contemplate the doings of their fallible fellow-men.

156

'The Squire's pretty springe, considering his weight,' said Mr
Macey, 'and he stamps uncommon well. . . . The parson's nimble
enough, but he hasn't got much of a leg: it's a bit too thick down'ard,
and his knees might be a bit nearer wi'out damage; but he might do
worse, he might do worse. Though he hasn't that grand way o'
waving his hand as the Squire has.'

GEORGE ELIOT (1819—1880)

SHEEP AND LAMBS

Methodists

119.   'You a parson, a shepherd of the flock, to come here,' she
            vociferated, 'and insult a poor woman like me (because I
called her 'beldame'). You will smart for this I assure you, I assure
you.' Tyler's wife, a very rank Methodist, who was in the house, then
began to join in the contest and asked whether I was not ashamed of
myself to call such names: that I might talk about canting Methodists,
but there never was a Churchman like me in a house but the Devil
was there also. I then said 'woman, such expressions I might make
you answer for in the Ecclesiastical Court, if you were not infinitely
beneath my notice.' Her husband then came in and compelled her
to go back to his own home, but not before she had retorted in the
greatest rage, 'Why, you called Mrs Smallcombe worse; you said she
was a "Beldame." ' I asked her what she supposed was meant by
that? And when I explained that it meant a scold, both she and
Smallcombe's wife became more tranquil, and said they had
supposed it meant something much worse.

I particularise these absurd scenes, not only because they are
worth recording as curiosities but, in another point of view, they are
indices of the malignity of these sectarists. Both Smallcombe and
this Tyler's wife gave the same pious expressions towards the clergy:
the one that parsons would howl in hell, and the other that where
there was a Churchman like me in a house there was the Devil. I am
heartily sick of the flock over which I am nominated and placed;
instead of being a shepherd, as I told the methodistical beldame
when she twitted me with the name, I am in fact a pig driver; I despise
myself most thoroughly for suffering irritation from such vermin.
Leaving these scenes of discord, I endeavoured to tranquillise my
mind by visiting those more softened by sickness and sorrow, and to
converse with those who do indeed need assistance.

JOHN SKINNER (1772—1839)

120.   Joshua Rann, the parish clerk, pays a surprise visit to the non-
            resident rector Mr Irwine.

'Well, Joshua, anything the matter at Hayslope, that you've come over this damp morning?... Have the thieves been at church lead again?'

'Thieves! no, sir,—an' yet, as I may say, it is thieves, an' a-thievin' the church, too. It's the Methodisses as is like to get th' upper hand i' th' parish, if your reverence an' his honour, Squire Donnithorne, doesna think well to say the word an' forbid it. Not as I'm a dictatin' to you, sir; I'm not forgettin' myself so far as to be wise above my betters. Howiver, whether I'm wise or no, that's neither here nor there, but what I've got to say—as the young Methodis woman, as is at Mester Poyser's, was a-preachin' an' a-prayin' on the Green ... last night; an' she's laid hold o' Chad's Bess, as the girl's been i' fits welly iver sin'.'

'Well, Bessy Cranage is a hearty-looking lass, I dare say she'll come round again, Joshua. Did anybody else go into fits?'

'No, sir, I canna say as they did. But there's no knowin' what'll come, if we're t' have such preachins as that agoin' on ivery week—there'll be no livin' i' th' village. For them Methodisses make folks believe as if they take a mug o' drink extry, an' make theirselves a bit comfortable, they'll have to go to hell for 't as sure as they're born....'

'Well, what's your advice, Joshua? What do you think should be done?'

'Well, your reverence, I'm not for takin' any measures again' the young woman.... But there's that Will Maskery, sir, as is the rampageousest Methodis as can be, an' I make no doubt it was him as stirred up th' young woman to preach last night, an' he'll be a-bringin' other folks to preach from Treddles'on, if his comb isn't cut a bit; an' I think as he should be let know as he isna t'have the makin' an' mendin' o' church carts an' implemens, let alone stayin' i' that house an' yard, as is Squire Donnithorne's... and what's worse, he's been heard to say very unbecomin' words about your reverence; for I could bring them as 'ud swear as he called you a "dumb dog," an' a "idle shepherd." You'll forgi'e me for sayin' such things over again.'

'Better not, better not, Joshua. Let evil words die as soon as they're spoken.... But it wouldn't become wise people, like you and me, to be making a fuss about trifles, as if we thought the Church was in danger because Will Maskery lets his tongue wag rather foolishly, or a young woman talks in a serious way to a handful of people on the Green. We must "live and let live," Joshua, in religion as well as in other things. You go on doing your duty, as parish clerk and sexton, as well as you've always done it, and making those capital thick boots for your neighbours, and things won't go far wrong in Hayslope, depend upon it.'

'Your reverence is very good to say so; an I'm sensable as, you not livin' i' the parish, there's more upo' my shoulders.'

'To be sure; and you must mind and not lower the Church in people's eyes by seeming to be frightened about it for a little thing, Joshua. I shall trust to your good sense, now, to take no notice at all of what Will Maskery says, either about you or me. You and your neighbours can go on taking your pot of beer soberly, when you've done your day's work, like good churchmen; and if Will Maskery doesn't like to join you, but to go to a prayer-meeting at Treddleston instead, let him; that's no business of yours, so long as he doesn't hinder you from doing what you like.'

GEORGE ELIOT (1819—1880)

121.   Bullhampton is very quiet. There is no special trade in the place. Its interests are altogether agricultural. It has no newspaper. Its tendencies are altogether conservative. It is a good deal given to religion; and the Primitive Methodists have a very strong holding there, although in all Wiltshire there is not a clergyman more popular in his own parish than the Rev. Frank Fenwick. He himself, in his inner heart, rather likes his rival, Mr Puddleham, the dissenting minister; because Mr Puddleham is an earnest man, who, inspite of the intensity of his ignorance, is efficacious among the poor. But Mr Fenwick is bound to keep up the fight; and Mr Puddleham considers it to be his duty to put down Mr Fenwick and the Church Establishment altogether. . . .

The strangest and most important piece of business going on at this time in Bullhampton was the building of a new chapel or

161

tabernacle,—the people called it a Salem,—for Mr Puddleham. The first word as to the errection reached Mr Fenwick's ears from Grimes, the builder and carpenter, who, meeting him in Bullhampton Street, pointed out to him a bit of spare ground just opposite the vicarage gates,—a morsel of a green on which no building had ever yet stood, and told him that the Marquis had given it for a chapel. 'Indeed,' said Fenwick. 'I hope it may be convenient and large enough for them. All the same, I wish it had been a little farther from my gate.' This he said in a cheery tone, showing thereby considerable presence of mind. That such a building should be so placed was a trial to him, and he knew at once that the spot must have been selected to annoy him. Doubtless, the land in question was the property of the Marquis of Trowbridge. When he came to think of it, he had no doubt on the matter. Nevertheless, the small semi-circular piece of grass immediately opposite to his own swinging gate, looked to all the world as though it were an appendage of the Vicarage. A cottage built there would have been offensive; but a staring brick Methodist chapel, with the word Salem inserted in large letters over the door, would, as he was aware, flout him every time he left or entered his garden.... When he heard those tidings, and saw what would be the effect of the building, it seemed to him almost impossible that a Marquis could condescend to such revenge. He went at once to Mr Puddleham, and learned from him that Grime's story was true. This had been in December. After Christmas, the foundations were to be begun at once, said Mr Puddleham, so that the brickwork might go on as soon as the frosts were over. Mr Puddleham was in high spirits, and expressed a hope that he should be in his new chapel by next August.

ANTHONY TROLLOPE (1815—1882)

Schools

122. The Rev. William Davy founded a school at Lustleigh a little while before his death. The schoolhouse has a tablet in the wall, with the date of 1825 and then these words, 'Built by subscription and endowed with Lowton Meadow in Moreton for supporting a school for ever by the Rev. William Davy curate of this parish.' His motives were set forth in his *Apology for giving Lowton Meadow to the Parish of Lustleigh*, a leaflet that he printed with his own printing press. 'Whereas from my long service in that church I have a strong regard and hearty desire for its present and future welfare, and being from repeated proofs too unhappily convinced of the uneconomical and profligate disposition of my immediate successors, and being willing in my lifetime to do the greatest and most lasting good with the little property I have in fee, I do hereby with the consent of my son (who by good conduct and kind providence is sufficiently provided for) offer to give to the officiating minister and churchwardens of the parish of Lustleigh all that one close or meadow called Morice or Lowton Meadow in Moreton Hampstead to have and to hold the same with the rents and profits thereof from and after the 25th of March 1824 in trust for ever for the support and maintenance of a school for poor children in the parish of Lustleigh aforesaid in the house to be erected in the parish town for that purpose.'

CECIL TORR (1857—1928)

123. The Reverend Gerald Partridge has been vicar of Fairacre, and its adjoining parish of Beech Green, for only four years, and so is looked upon as a foreigner by most of his parishioners. His energetic wife is as brisk and practical as he is gentle and vague. He is chairman of the managers of Fairacre school and comes in every Friday morning to take a scripture lesson with the older children.

On this morning, he carried a list of hymns, which he asked me to teach the children during the term, and I said I would look through them. He sighed at my guarded answer, for he knew as well as I did that not all the hymns would be considered suitable by me for teaching to children. His weakness for the metaphysical poets led him into choosing quite inexplicable hymns about showers and brides, with lines like:

Rend each man's temple-veil and bid it fall,

or, worse still, Milton's poems set as hymns, containing such lines as:

And speckled vanity
Will sicken soon and die,
And leprous sin will melt from earthly mould,

all of which may be very fine in its way but is quite beyond the comprehension of the pupils here. The vicar smiles and nods his mild old head when I protest.

'Very well, my dear, very well. Just as you think best. Let us leave that hymn until they are older.' And then he meanders away to talk to the children, leaving me feeling a bully and browbeater.

He drank his tea and then started up his car, setting off, very slowly and carefully, down the road to his vicarage.

MISS READ (1913—   )

124.   Every morning at ten o'clock the Rector arrived to take the older children for Scripture. He was a parson of the old school; a commanding figure, tall and stout, with white hair, ruddy cheeks and an aristocratically beaked nose, and he was as far as possible removed by birth, education and worldly circumstances from the lambs of his flock. He spoke to them from a great height, physical, mental and spiritual. 'To order myself lowly and reverently before my betters' was the clause he underlined in the Church Catechism, for had he not been divinely appointed pastor and master to those little rustics and was it not one of his chief duties to teach them to realize this? As a man, he was kindly disposed—a giver of blankets and coals at Christmas and of soup and milk puddings to the sick.

FLORA THOMPSON (1876—1947)

164

125.   The day was done, and Fancy was again in the school-house.
        About five o'clock it began to rain, and in rather a dull frame
of mind she wandered into the schoolroom for want of something
better to do. . . . Then there arose a soft series of raps no louder than
the tappings of a distant woodpecker, and barely distinct enough to
reach her ears. She composed herself and flung open the door.

In the porch stood Mr Maybold.

There was a warm flush upon his face and a bright flash in his eyes
which made him look handsomer than she had ever seen him
before.

'Good-evening, Miss Day.'

'Good-evening, Mr Maybold,' she said, in a strange state of
mind. . . . Without another word being spoken by either he came
into the schoolroom, shut the door, and moved close to her. Once
inside the expression of his face was no more discernible by reason
of the increasing dusk of the evening.

'I want to speak to you,' he then said; 'seriously—on a perhaps
unexpected subject, but one which is all the world to me—I don't
know what it may be to you, Miss Day.'

No reply.

'Fancy, I have come to ask you if you will be my wife?'

As a person who has been idly amusing himself with rolling a
snowball might start at finding he had set in motion an avalanche, so
did Fancy start at these words from the young vicar. . . .

'I cannot, I cannot, Mr Maybold—I cannot! Don't ask me!' she said.

'Don't answer in a hurry!' he entreated. 'And do listen to me. This is
no sudden feeling on my part. I have loved you for more than six
months! Perhaps my late interest in teaching the children here has
not been so single-minded as it seemed. You will understand my
motive—like me better, perhaps, for honestly telling you that I have
struggled against my emotion continually, because I have thought
that it was not well for me to love you! But I resolved to struggle no
longer.

THOMAS HARDY (1840 -1928)

126.   Nervously therefore I pushed open the door of the saloon
bar of the Cheerful Smile that evening and entered. About
four or five men were sitting round the room and one youngish
woman was perched, with her legs crossed, on a stool at the bar. She
was reading a newspaper.

'Evening sir,' said the man behind the bar. I took him to be the
landlord.

'Good evening. Could I have a—a cider, please?' I hoped my
uncertainty was not too noticeable. If my visit was to appear natural, I
should at least know what I wanted.

While the landlord was drawing the cider, the woman looked up
from her paper and smiled at me. 'Passing through?' she asked
pleasantly.

Before I could reply the landlord corrected, 'It's our new vicar.'
Then, as though he'd hardly expected to see me on his premises,
'You are, aren't you, sir?'

I nodded and the woman looked at me with new interest.

'Good for you,' she said. 'This is one way of getting to know your
parishioners!' She had a well-educated voice, and the cut of her
costume was excellent. Her name was Mrs Atwell, and I could
cheerfully have spent the rest of the evening sitting on the stool next
to her. She had a way with her—enlisting my aid with her crossword
puzzle, steadying my hand as I clumsily attempted to light her
cigarette, and getting me to give far more information about myself
than I normally did. . . .

'You know,' I said to Mrs Atwell, 'I really ought to move around
and speak to some of the others.'

'Forget it, enjoy yourself. I'll tell you who they all are.'

'That would be cheating.'

'Would it? Not if you were here for pleasure. You should relax
sometimes, you know. "All work and no play. . ." I think you should
come here again one evening and leave your work behind you.'

'Without my dog collar?'

'Without your dog collar,' she mimicked. 'You're only going to talk to these old codgers out of a sense of duty.'

'Oh, no, I —' She was right, in a way, of course. I did have an ulterior motive. 'Well, actually, I'm hoping something may happen before I leave.'

She looked amused. 'How exciting! Are you going to preach a sermon?'

'Good heavens, no.'

'A miracle, then? Well . . . you're a change from the usual run.' She gave me a look. 'You may see me at St Hilda's yet.'

I smiled quizzically. 'You make *that* sound like a miracle.' Sliding from my stool and hoping that the cider wasn't going to my head, I added, 'I'd be very pleased to see it come true.'

It was interesting, I thought, how intrigued some people became if a clergyman talks to them in a perfectly ordinary fashion without pushing religion at them. I could almost hear Mrs Atwell thinking 'What's his game?'

Terrified at the possibility of a snub, I spoke to the man nearest to the bar. He greeted me with warmth, leaping up and saying that he was the bell-ringer at St Hilda's.

'This is nice, sir,' he beamed. 'I've been wanting to talk to you ever since you came in, but I didn't dare.'

'Why not?' I asked.

'Well, it was the last vicar. He wasn't too keen on the drink . . .' He smiled happily. 'But of course, I can see you're all for it.'

JAMES INSIGHT (1916—   )

127.   The day after Daphne left, Tom had strolled into the pub, not so much to have a drink—he was not the type of rector who mingled easily with the village people, even in pursuit of local history—as to have a word with Mr Spears, the landlord, who supervised the cutting of the churchyard grass. For some time now the cow-parsley round the graves had been over and given place to what could only be described as hay. Something must obviously be done about it.

167

'Good morning,' Tom said.

'Morning, rector.'

'About time the grass was cut again,' Tom said, in what he hoped was a pleasant, easy tone of voice. He had been practising how he would put it on his way to the pub. He had ordered a half of lager, aware that it was probably regarded as a 'ladies drink', and sat down in a corner. Then he had brought out his remark about the grass, but there was no answer. He had forgotten that Mr Spears was sometimes a little deaf. He took a sip of lager and tried again. 'I was wondering about that grass,' he said more loudly.

'A wonderful thing, grass,' said Mr Spears. 'Reminds me of that hymn.'

The old lines came back to Tom,

> Within the churchyard, side by side,
> Are many long low graves;
> And some have stones set over them,
> On some the green grass waves.

Presumably that was the hymn he meant, not one they ever sang now; 'morbid', whether classed with hymns 'For the Young', as it was in A and M, or anywhere else. Tom couldn't remember whether it had been included in the English Hymnal, he thought probably not; it had some questionable lines . . . .

Mr Spears was saying something further about grass, either that he had intended to cut it but had no scythe, or that he hadn't been able to get round to doing anything about it yet. Tom's diversion into Mrs Alexander's hymn had caused him to miss the main point of what was being said.

BARBARA PYM (1913—1980)

128. No sooner had the little party quitted the Rectory gates than the sounds of tumult burst upon them. The 'Barley Mow' lay but a furlong off, and as they approached, suggestive shouts reached their ears, one or two voices, notably shrill feminine ones, rising above the rest. . . .

168

Then above the scuffle and confusion, *mêlée* of village Montagus and Capulets, Guelph and Ghiberlin, were heard alarming shouts of 'Murder! Help! Police!' with 'Seize him! Give it 'em! Punch his head!' and the like, half smothering the remonstrances of outsiders and the frightened cries of the children.

Not one whit daunted . . . the burly Rector, with lifted bludgeon, forced his way into the thick of the fight.

'Churchwarden!' he thundered out—his voice was by far the most powerful in the parish—'I call on you in the Queen's name to do your duty. Blockheads! blackguards! besotted idiots, that ever I should own such a lot of parishioners! Hands off! Desist! Quiet! Do you suppose that because the parish constable, by the grace of God, is confined to his bed, the law of the land is to be set at naught? I'd have you to know then, one and all, churchgoers and ranters—a pretty set all of you—I'd have you to know that the authority of your minister is not confined to the pulpit. Lay about with your cudgel, churchwarden, I take upon myself all responsibility. Home, meek as lambs, every mother's son of you, or it's not the ringleaders alone, I'll warrant you, who'll find their way to the treadmill.'

The unexpected onslaught had immediate effect. Mr Pascoe's sudden appearance and stentorian shouts sobered brawlers, separated combatants, cowed the bullies and silenced the women. Just as a crowd melts away when overtaken by a hailstorm, so the Largess-spenders now dispersed; some scuttled in one direction, others slunk away in another, all with the utmost possible dispatch getting beyond reach of the Rector's knobstick and vituperations.

It was the latter that most impressed. In these early days villagers might be meeteners, indifferentists, infidels, so-called, but a certain kind of divinity did hedge a parson. The least devotional, the most uncompromising Noncon., the openly irreverent, in the person of a clergyman respected much that he would have found it difficult to define . . . .

A few minutes later and the 'Barley Mow' was barred, shuttered, silent.

M. Betham-Edwards (1836—1919)

Conflict

129.   Mr Henry Moule, the Vicar of Fordington for nearly half a
       century, met me at the Dorchester Station, pointed out to me
the great Roman amphitheatre, Maiden Castle, the vallum of the
Roman camp, and took me round the beautiful avenues of luxuriant
sycamore and chestnut which surround and adorn the town. . . .

The Vicar told me part of the history of the politics of Fordington,
his troubles with the Dorchester people and his struggles with the
Council of the Duchy of Cornwall to which the parish of Fordington
belongs and from which with great difficulty he has at length wrung
some acknowledgement and help in money and improvements.

When the Vicar first came to Fordington he was instrumental, he
said, in putting down some low bad races held near Dorchester. This
made him very unpopular. For five years none of his family or flock
would go into Dorchester without being insulted and baa-ed after
like sheep. Twenty or thirty young men stood at the Church gates
each Sunday and insulted the pastor and his congregation as they
went into Church. And every year all the shrubs and flowers in the
garden were rooted up and placed together in the middle of the
lawn. All the opposition however had been lived down long ago and
now the Vicar seems universally and deservedly respected . . . .

Then the Vicar of Fordington told us of the state of things in his
parish when he first came to it nearly half a century ago. No man had
ever been known to receive the Holy Communion except the
parson, the clerk and the sexton. There were 16 women
communicants and most of them went away when he refused to pay
them for coming.

FRANCIS KILVERT (1840—1872)

130.   Years ago, when first he had come to the parish, it was with
       determination to improve the lot of those in his care. . . .
Wherever people were gathered together, be it for sport or be it in
earnest, thither he went, and with a set purpose beforehand made it
felt that he was there. He did not remain a passive spectator in the

background, but came as prominently to the front as was compatible with due courtesy.

When the cloth was cleared at the ordinary in the market town, and the farmers proceeded to the business of their club, or chamber, he appeared in the doorway, and quietly took a seat not far from the chair. If the discussion were purely technical he said nothing; if it touched, as it frequently did, upon social topics, such as those that arose out of education, of the labour question, of the position of the farmer apart from the mere ploughing and sowing, then he delivered his opinion. When the local agricultural exhibition was proceeding and the annual dinner was held he sat at the social board, and presently made his speech. The village benefit club held its *fête*—he was there too, perhaps presiding at the dinner, and addressed the assembled men. He took part in the organisation of the cottage flower show; excited himself earnestly about the allotments and the winter coal club, and endeavoured to provide the younger people with amusements that did not, in his opinion, lead to evil—supporting cricket and such games as might be played apart from gambling and liquor.

This is but the barest catalogue of his work in those early days; there was nothing that arose, no part of the life of the village and the countryside, to which he did not set his hand . . . .

He was not permitted to pursue this course unmolested; there were parties in the village that silently opposed his every footstep. Had the battle been open it would have been easier to win it, but it was concealed. The Church is not often denounced from the housetop, but it is certainly denounced under the roof. The poor and ignorant were instructed that the Church was their greatest enemy, the upholder of tyranny, the instrument of their subjection, synonymous with lowered wages and privation, more iniquitous than the landowner . . . . The poor man had but a few shillings a week, and the clergyman was the friend of the farmer, who reduced his wages—the Church owned millions and millions sterling. How self-evident, therefore, that the Church was the cottager's enemy . . . .!

Another party was for pure secularism. This was not so numerously represented, but had increased of recent years. From political motives both of these silently opposed the parson. Nor were the poor and ignorant alone among the ranks of his foes. There were some tenant farmers among them, but their attitude was not so coarsely antagonistic. They took no action against, but they did not assist, him. So that, although, as he went about the parish, he was not greeted with hisses, the clergyman was full well aware that his activity was a thorn in the side of many. They reproached him with interfering in matters outside his cloth; and gradually, as the keen edge of his benevolence wore off, he took to the seclusion of the parsonage.

RICHARD JEFFERIES (1849—1887)

131.   The chief members of Mellstock parish choir were standing in a group in front of Mr Penny's workshop in the lower village. . . . They talked with deliberate gesticulations to Mr Penny, enthroned in the shadow of the interior. . . .

'He's a poor gawk-hammer. Look at his sermon yesterday.'

'His sermon was well enough, a very good guessable sermon, only he couldn't put it into words and speak it. That's all was the matter wi' the sermon. He hadn't been able to get it past his pen . . . .'

'He's no spouter—that must be said, 'a b'lieve.'

' 'Tis a terrible muddle sometimes with the man, as afar as spout do go,' said Spinks.

'Well, we'll say nothing about that,' the tranter answered; 'for I don't believe 'twill make a penneth o' difference to we poor martels here or hereafter whether his sermons be good or bad, my sonnies.'

Mr Penny made another hole with his awl, pushed in the thread, and looked up and spoke again at the extension of arms.

' 'Tis his goings-on, souls, that's what it is.' He clenched his features for an Herculean addition to the ordinary pull, and continued, 'The first thing he done when he came here was to be hot and strong about church business.'

'True,' said Spinks; 'that was the very first thing he done.'

Mr Penny, having now been offered the ear of the assembly, accepted it, ceased stitching, swallowed an unimportant quantity of air as if it were a pill, and continued:

172

'The next thing he do do is to think about altering the church, until he found 'twould be a matter o' cost and what not, and then not to think no more about it.'

'True: that was the next thing he done.'

'And the next thing was to tell the young chaps that they were not on no account to put their hats in the christening font during service.'

'True.'

'And then 'twas this, and then 'twas that, and now 'tis. . . to turn us out of the quire neck and crop.'

Mrs Penny came to the door at this point in the discussion . . . .

'It must be owned he's not all there,' she replied in a general way to the fragments of talk she had heard from indoors. 'Far below poor Mr Grinham' (the late vicar).

'Ay, there was this to be said for he, that you were quite sure he'd never come mumbudgeting to see ye, just as you were in the middle of your work, and put you out with his fuss and trouble about ye.'

'Never. But as for this new Mr Maybold, though he mid be a very well-intending party in that respect, he's unbearable; for as to sifting your cinders, scrubbing your floors, or emptying your slops, why, you can't do it. I assure you I've not been able to empty them for several days, unless I throw 'em up the chimley or out of winder; for as sure as the sun you meet him at the door, coming to ask how you are, and 'tis such a confusing thing to meet a gentleman at the door when ye are in the mess o' washing.'

' 'Tis only for the want of knowing better, poor gentleman,' said the tranter. 'His meaning's good enough. Ay, your pa'son comes by fate: 'tis heads or tails, like pitch-halfpenny, and no choosing; so we must take en as he is, my sonnies, and thank God he's no worse, I suppose. . . .'

'Ah, Mr Grinham was the man! said Bowman. 'Why, he never troubled us wi' a visit from year's end to year's end. You might go anywhere, do anything: you'd be sure never to see him.'

'Yes; he was a right sensible pa'son,' said Michael. 'He never entered our poor door but once in his life, and that was to tell my poor wife—ay, poor soul, dead and gone now, as we all shall!—that as she was such a' old aged person, and lived so far from the church, he didn't at all expect her to come any more to the service.'

'And 'a was a very jinerous gentleman about choosing the psalms and hymns o' Sundays. "Confound ye," says he, "blare and scrape what ye will, but don't bother me . . . !" '

'And there's this man never letting us have a bit o' peace . . . .'

'No sooner had he got here than he found the font wouldn't hold water, as it hadn't for years off and on; and when I told him that Mr Grinham never minded, but used to spet upon his vinger and christen 'em just as well, 'a said, "Good Heavens! Send for a workman immediate. What place have I come to!" Which was no compliment to us, come to that.'

THOMAS HARDY (1840—1928)

132.   To count the years he was old: he had been vicar of Coombe for half a century, but he was a young man still and had never had a day's illness in his life—he did not know what a headache was. He smoked with me, and to prove that he was not a total abstainer he drank my health in a glass of port wine—very good wine . . . .

He took me to the church—one of the tiniest churches in the country, just the right size for a church in a tiny village, and assured me that he had never once locked the door in his fifty years—day and night it was open to anyone to enter. . . . He had never locked it, but once in fifty years it had been locked against him by the churchwardens. This happened in the days of the Joseph Arch agitation, when the agricultural labourer's condition was being hotly discussed throughout the country. The vicar's heart was stirred, for he knew better than most how hard these conditions were at Coombe and in the surrounding parishes. He took up the subject and preached on it in his own pulpit in a way that offended the landowners and alarmed the farmers in the district. The churchwardens, who were farmers, then locked him out of his church, and for two or three weeks there was no public worship in the parish of Coombe. Doubtless their action was applauded by all the substantial men in the neighbourhood; the others who lived in the cottages and were unsubstantial didn't matter. That storm blew

174

over, but its consequences endured, one being that the inflammatory parson continued to be regarded with cold disapproval by the squires and their larger tenants. But the vicar himself was unrepentant and unashamed; on the contrary, he gloried in what he had said and done, and was proud to be able to relate that a quarter of a century later one of the two men who had taken that extreme course said to him, 'We locked you out of your own church, but years have brought me to another mind about that question. I see it in a different light now and know that you were right and we were wrong.'

W.H. HUDSON (1841—1922)

PIKE

5. WORK AND RECREATION

Naturalist

133.   The Reverend Charles Butler studied at Magdalen College
        Oxford from 1579 to 1587, where he finally graduated as
Master of Arts. He had been Chorister of Magdalen during his
student years and studied music with more than usual assiduity. His
first recorded appointment, in 1595, gave him the double
responsibility of the small parish of Nately Scures and of the Mastership of the Holy Ghost School, at Basingstoke.

The Schoolmaster was a priest appointed to perform divine service in the Chapel and 'to instruct the young men and boys of the town
in religion and literature'. For this Butler's salary amounted to twelve
pounds per annum. He rented for twelve shillings per annum the
hay from the cemetery. It is likely, here in Basingstoke, driven by
economic necessity, that bees first came into his life. The Mastership
ended in 1600 when he was appointed to the living of Wootton St
Lawrence. . . .

Once settled at Wootton, Butler was able to concentrate on his
observations and writings about bees. The resulting book was published in 1609 under the title 'The Feminine Monarchie or Treatise
concerning Bees and the due ordering of them', in which for the first
time real rules for the 'ordering' were based on his own practical
experience and not on the precepts of Aristotle. The title of the book
proclaimed that a colony of bees was headed by a Queen and not by
a King as was hitherto the general consensus.

FRANK VERNON (1922—1986)

134.　A country parson whose senses were attuned to Nature was
in an ideal situation to pursue the hobby of naturalist, and
nineteenth-century natural science in its broadest aspects owes a
good deal to the patient industry of these cheerful, unpaid research
assistants. . : .

Among these esteemed names we must place the Rev. Octavius
Pickard-Cambridge, rector of Bloxworth in Dorset, who may fairly
be described as the 'Father of British Spiders', although he did not
limit himself to spiders but interested himself in all insects and flora.
The fame of this Dorset clergyman was worldwide in his life-time
and his work is still recognized as being of permanent value. Dr W.S.
Bristowe, naturalist and author believes that we know more about
British spiders and their habits than people of any other country in
the world, and he attributes this to the work and influence of
Octavius Pickard-Cambridge. . . . .

His own scientific researches and studies were carried out at virtually no cost, as he walked or bicycled around Dorset to get specimens, and his notes, drawings and classifications were made in a
specially converted outbuilding of the rectory, christened the 'Den'.
Family and friends were under standing orders to send to Bloxworth
any interesting specimens. . . .

By 1880 Octavius had published almost eighty scientific papers
on spiders alone, in addition to about forty on antiquarian subjects,
on meteorology, mammals, reptiles, birds, lepidoptera and general
entomology. He was now in his early fifties, vigorous in his parish
work, dedicated to science, and for the following thirty years he
maintained an unflagging correspondence with scientists all over
the world, and willingly identified and classified other people's specimens, with the sole condition that he should be allowed to keep one
perfect specimen for his own collection which was destined for
Oxford University after his death. He made that proviso because he
had discovered very early that other collectors were frequently less
careful than he in preserving their specimens intact over the years.
Octavius had meticulously high standards, unlike some amateur scientists whom he sardonically called 'the goodness gracious scientists'.　　　　　　　　　　　　　　　　　　B. COLLOMS (1919—　)

135.   The Reverend Gilbert White (1720-93) lived for almost all
his life in the secluded Hampshire village of Selborne, and it
was this quiet and obscure place that provided most of the subject
matter for the book that has become a classic of English writing, *The
Natural History and Antiquities of Selborne*. As White's college
friend John Mulso accurately predicted, the book brought fame
both to its author and to his native village.

Gilbert White was born in the vicarage in Selborne on 18 July
1720, when his grandfather, the Reverend Gilbert White senior
(1650-1728), was vicar of St Mary's church. This living was a gift of
Magdalen College, Oxford, and therefore the naturalist (the
Reverend Gilbert White junior), being a graduate of another college,
could never hold the title of vicar of Selborne. However, he was able
to serve as curate on a number of occasions. . . .

He also retained his college Fellowship and served Oriel College
as Junior Proctor in 1751; at a later date he made an unsuccessful
application for the post of Provost. It was comparatively late in life, in
1757, that Gilbert White accepted an Oriel College living at
Moreton Pinkney in Northamptonshire. Rather against the wishes
of the college, he did not work the living himself, but put a curate in
his place and continued to live and serve as a curate in
Hampshire. . . .

All the White brothers shared an interest in natural history and, by
regular correspondence and visits, they provided Gilbert with
considerable help and outside contacts, in particular brother
Benjamin who was a publisher and bookseller in London and
responsible for many important natural history books of the
eighteenth century. Notable naturalists from other parts of Britain
frequently visited Benjamin White's business, and this was the
source of Gilbert's contacts with the Honourable Daines Barrington
and the eminent zoologist Thomas Pennant, which led to the
remarkable correspondence on which *The Natural History of
Selborne* was based. . . .

In both series of letters, Gilbert White covered a wide range of
topics, and he also put forward views on his approach to the study of
natural history. He strongly believed in the value of first-hand

observation in the field and it was his opinion that many naturalists spent too much time in the study. White's prime interest was in the behaviour of animals and he had comparatively little regard for the traditional work of zoologists and botanists who did, and intended to do, no more than give names to new species. In considering the characteristics for recognizing a bird, White pointed out the significance of behaviour, mannerisms and song in addition to features of the plumage. Gilbert White was a pioneer in behavioural science, in field work and also in the concentrated study of a small area.

GILBERT WHITE (1720—1793)

Scholar

136. Mr Abraham Adams was an excellent scholar. He was a perfect master of the Greek and Latin languages; to which he added a great share of knowledge in the Oriental tongues; and could read and translate French, Italian, and Spanish. He had applied many years to the most severe study, and had treasured up a fund of learning rarely to be met with in a university. He was, besides, a man of good sense, good parts, and good nature; but was at the same time as entirely ignorant of the ways of this world as an infant just entered into it could possibly be. As he had never any intention to deceive, so he never suspected such a design in others. He was generous, friendly, and brave to an excess; but simplicity was his characteristick. . . .

His virtue, and his other qualifications, as they rendered him equal to his office, so they made him an agreeable and valuable companion, and had so much endeared and well recommended him to a bishop, that at the age of fifty he was provided with a handsome income of twenty-three pounds a year; which, however, he could not make any great figure with, because he lived in a dear country, and was a little encumbered with a wife and six children.

HENRY FIELDING (1707—1754)

137. 'Palestine soup!' said the Reverend Doctor Opimian, dining with his friend Squire Gryll; 'a curiously complicated misnomer. We have an excellent old vegetable, the artichoke, of which we eat the head; we have another of subsequent introduction, of which we eat the root, and which we also call artichoke, because it resembles the first in flavour, although, *me judice*, a very inferior affair. This last is a species of the helianthus, or sunflower genus of the *Syngenesia frustranea* class of plants. It is therefore a girasol, or turn-to-the-sun. From this girasol we have made Jerusalem, and from the Jerusalem artichoke we make Palestine soup. . . .'

Miss Gryll. 'You and my uncle, doctor, get up a discussion on everything that presents itself. . . . You have run half round the world *à propos* of the soup. What say you to the fish?'

The Revd Dr Opimian. 'Premising that this is a remarkably fine slice of salmon, there is much to said about fish: but not in the way of misnomers. Their names are single and simple. Perch, sole, cod, eel, carp, char, skate, tench, trout, brill, bream, pike, and many others, plain monosyllables: salmon, dory, turbot, gudgeon, lobster, whitebait, grayling, haddock, mullet, herring, oyster, sturgeon, flounder, turtle, plain dissyllables: only two trisyllables worth naming, anchovy and mackerel; unless any one should be disposed to stand up for halibut, which, for my part, I have excommunicated.'

THOMAS LOVE PEACOCK (1785—1866)

138.   Then came the Author-Rector: his delight
    Was all in books; to read them, or to write:
    Women and men he strove alike to shun,
    And hurried homeward when his tasks were done:
    Courteous enough, but careless what he said,
    For points of learning he reserved his head;
    And when addressing either poor or rich,
    He knew no better than his cassock which:
    He, like an osier, was of pliant kind,
    Erect by nature, but to bend inclined;
    Not like a creeper falling to the ground,
    Or meanly catching on the neighbours round:—
    Careless was he of surplice, hood, and band,—
    And kindly took them as they came to hand:
    Nor, like the doctor, wore a world of hat,
    As if he sought for dignity in that:
    He talk'd, he gave, but not with cautious rules:—
    Nor turn'd from gipsies, vagabonds, or fools;
    It was his nature, but they thought it whim,
    And so our beaux and beauties turn'd from him:
    Of questions, much he wrote, profound and dark,—

How spake the serpent, and where stopp'd the ark;
From what far land the Queen of Sheba came;
Who Salem's priest, and what his father's name;
He made the Song of Songs its mysteries yield,
And Revelations, to the world, reveal'd.
He sleeps i' the aisle,—but not a stone records
His name or fame, his actions or his words.

GEORGE CRABBE (1754—1832)

139.　'I must observe, that I am not entirely without the means of seeing what clergymen are, being at this present time the guest of my own brother, Dr Grant. And though Dr Grant is most kind and obliging to me, and though he is really a gentleman, and I dare say a good scholar and clever, and often preaches good sermons, and is very respectable, I see him to be an indolent selfish bon vivant, who must have his palate consulted in every thing, who will not stir a finger for the convenience of any one, and who, moreover, if the cook makes a blunder, is out of humour with his excellent wife. To own the truth, Henry and I were partly driven out this very evening, by a disappointment about a green goose, which he could not get the better of. My poor sister was forced to stay and bear it.'

'I do not wonder at your disapprobation, upon my word. It is a great defect of temper, made worse by a very faulty habit of self-indulgence; and to see your sister suffering from it, must be exceedingly painful to such feelings as yours. Fanny, it goes against us. We cannot attempt to defend Dr Grant.'

'No,' replied Fanny, 'but we need not give up his profession for all that; because, whatever profession Dr Grant had chosen, he would have taken a—not good temper into it; and as he must either in the navy or army have had a great many more people under his command than he has now, I think more would have been made unhappy by him as a sailor or soldier than as a clergyman. Besides, I cannot but suppose that whatever there may be to wish otherwise in Dr Grant, would have been in a greater danger of becoming worse in

183

a more active and worldly profession, where he would have had less time and obligation—where he might have escaped that knowledge of himself, the frequency, at least, of that knowledge which it is impossible he should escape as he is now. A man—a sensible man like Dr Grant, cannot be in the habit of teaching others their duty every week, cannot go to church twice every Sunday and preach such very good sermons in so good a manner as he does, without being the better for it himself. It must make him think, and I have no doubt that he oftener endeavours to restrain himself than he would if he had been any thing but a clergyman.'

JANE AUSTEN (1775—1817)

140. Tom Tulliver's sufferings during the first quarter he was at
       King's Lorton, under the distinguished care of the Rev.
Walter Stelling, were rather severe. . . .

Mr Stelling was a well-sized, broad chested man, not yet thirty, with flaxen hair standing erect, and large lightish-grey eyes, which were always very wide open; he had a sonorous bass voice, and an air of defiant self-confidence inclining to brazenness. He had entered on his career with great vigour, and intended to make a considerable impression on his fellow-men. The Rev. Walter Stelling was not a man who would remain among the 'inferior clergy' all his life. He had a true British determination to push his way in the world. As a school master, in the first place; for there were capital masterships of grammar-schools to be had, and Mr Stelling meant to have one of them. . . .

In short, Mr Stelling was a man who meant to rise in his profession, and to rise by merit, clearly, since he had no interest beyond what might be promised by a problematic relationship to a great lawyer who had not yet become Lord Chancellor. A clergyman who has such vigorous intentions naturally gets a little into debt at starting; it is not to be expected that he will live in the meagre style of a man who means to be a poor curate all his life, and if the few hundreds Mr Timpson advanced towards his daughter's fortune did not suffice for the purchase of handsome furniture, together with a stock of wine, a grand piano, and the laying out of a superior flower-garden, it followed in the most rigorous manner, either that these things must be procured by some other means, or else that the Rev. Mr Stelling must go without them—which last alternative would be an absurd procrastination of the fruits of success, where success was certain. . . .

But the immediate step to future success was to bring on Tom Tulliver during this first half-year; for by a singular coincidence, there had been some negotiation concerning another pupil from the same neighbourhood, and it might further a decision in Mr Stelling's favour, if it were understood that young Tulliver, who, Mr

Stelling observed in conjugal privacy, was rather a rough cub, had
made prodigious progress in a short time. It was on this ground that
he was severe with Tom about his lessons. . . . Not that Mr Stelling
was a harsh-tempered or unkind man—quite the contrary: he was
jocose with Tom at table, and corrected his provincialisms and his
deportment in the most playful manner; but poor Tom was only the
more cowed and confused by this double novelty, for he had never
been used to jokes like Mr Stelling's; and for the first time in his life he
had a painful sense that he was all wrong somehow. When Mr
Stelling said, as the roast-beef was being uncovered, 'Now, Tulliver!
which would you rather decline, roast-beef or the Latin for it?'—
Tom, to whom in his coolest moments a pun would have been a hard
nut, was thrown into a state of embarrassed alarm. . .: of course he
answered, 'Roast-beef', where upon there followed much laughter
and some practical joking with the plates, from which Tom gathered
that he had in some mysterious way refused beef, and, in fact, made
himself appear 'a silly'. If he could have seen a fellow-pupil undergo
these painful operations and survive them in good spirits, he might
sooner have taken them as a matter of course. But there are two
expensive forms of education, either of which a parent may procure
for his son by sending him as solitary pupil to a clergyman: one is, the
enjoyment of the reverend gentleman's undivided neglect; the
other is, the endurance of the reverend gentleman's undivided
attention. It was the latter privilege for which Mr Tulliver paid a high
price in Tom's initiatory months at King's Lorton.

GEORGE ELIOT (1819—1880)

141. Framley church stood immediately opposite to the chief
       entrance to Framley Court. . . . Beyond the church, but close
to it, were the boys' school and girls' school, two distinct buildings,
which owed their erection to Lady Lufton's energy. . . . And here the
road took a sudden turn to the left, turning, as it were, away from
Framley Court; and just beyond the turn was the vicarage, so that
there was a little garden path running from the back of the vicarage
grounds into the churchyard. . . .

186

Other village at Framley there was none. At the back of the Court, up one of those cross-roads, there was another small shop or two, and there was a very neat cottage residence, in which lived the widow of a former curate, another protégé of Lady Lufton's; and there was a big, staring, brick house, in which the present curate lived; but this was a full mile distant from the church, and farther from Framley Court, standing on that cross-road which runs from Framley Court in a direction away from the mansion. This gentleman, the Rev. Evan Jones, might, from his age, have been the vicar's father; but he had been for many years curate of Framley; and though he was personally disliked by Lady Lufton, as being Low Church in his principles, and unsightly in his appearance, nevertheless, she would not urge his removal. He had two or three pupils in that large brick house, and, if turned out from these and from his curacy, might find it difficult to establish himself elsewhere. On this account mercy was extended to the Rev. E. Jones, and, in spite of his red face and awkward big feet, he was invited to dine at Framley Court, with his plain daughter, once in every three months.

ANTHONY TROLLOPE (1815—1882)

142.   Parson Adams came to the house of parson Trulliber, whom
         he found stript into his waistcoat, with an apron on, and a pail
in his hand, just come from serving his hogs; for Mr Trulliber was a
parson on Sundays, but all the other six might more properly be
called a farmer. He occupied a small piece of land of his own, besides
which he rented a considerable deal more. His wife milked his cows,
managed his dairy, and followed the markets with butter and eggs.
The hogs fell chiefly to his care, which he carefully waited on at
home, and attended to fairs; on which occasion he was liable to
many jokes, his own size being, with much ale, rendered little inferior
to that of the beasts he sold. He was indeed one of the largest men
you should see, and could have acted the part of Sir John Falstaff
without stuffing. Add to this that the rotundity of his belly was
considerably increased by the shortness of his stature, his shadow
ascending very near as far in height, when he lay on his back, as when
he stood on his legs. His voice was loud and hoarse, and his accents
extremely broad. To complete the whole, he had a stateliness in his
gait, when he walked, not unlike that of a goose, only he stalked
slower.

Mr Trulliber, being informed that somebody wanted to speak with
him, immediately slipt off his apron and clothed himself in an old
night-gown, being the dress in which he always saw his company at
home. His wife, who informed him of Mr Adams's arrival, had made
a small mistake; for she had told her husband 'She believed there
was a man come for some of his hogs.' This supposition made Mr
Trulliber hasten with the utmost expedition to attend his guest. He
no sooner saw Adams than, not in the least doubting the cause of his
errand to be what his wife had imagined, he told him, 'He was come
in very good time; that he expected a dealer that very afternoon';
and added, 'they were all pure and fat, and upwards of twenty score
a-piece.' Adams answered, 'He believed he did not know him.' 'Yes,
yes,' cried Trulliber, 'I have seen you often at fair; why we have dealt
before now, mun, I warrant you. Yes, Yes,' cries he, 'I remember thy
face very well, but won't mention a word more till you have seen

them, though I have never sold thee a flitch of such bacon as is now in the stye.' Upon which he laid violent hands on Adams, and dragged him into the hog-stye, which was indeed but two steps from his parlour window. They were no sooner arrived here than he cry'd out, 'Do but handle them! step in, friend! art welcome to handle them, whether dost buy or no.' At which words, opening the gate, he pushed Adams into the pig-stye, insisting on it that he should handle them before he would talk one word with him.

Adams, whose natural complacence was beyond any artificial, was obliged to comply before he was suffered to explain himself; and, laying hold on one of their tails, the unruly beast gave such a sudden spring, that he threw poor Adams all along in the mire. Trulliber, instead of assisting him to get up, burst into a laughter, and, entering the stye, said to Adams, with some contempt, 'Why, dost not know how to handle a hog?' and was going to lay hold of one himself, but Adams, who thought he had carried his complacence far enough, was no sooner on his legs than he escaped out of the reach of the animals, and cried out, *'Nihil habeo cum porcis*: I am a clergyman, sir, and am not come to buy hogs.'

HENRY FIELDING (1707—1754)

143.   'The Hope Farm is not a stone's throw from here,' said the officious landlord, going to the window. 'If you carry your eye over yon bed of hollyhocks, over the damson-trees in the orchard yonder, you may see a stack of queer-like stone chimneys. Them is the Hope Farm chimneys: it's an old place, though Holman keeps it in good order.'

Mr Holdsworth had risen from the table with more promptitude than I had, and was standing by the window, looking. At the landlord's last words, he turned round, smiling—'it is not often that parsons know how to keep land in order, is it?'

'Beg pardon, sir, but I must speak as I find; and Minister Holman— we call the Church clergyman here "parson", sir; he would be a bit jealous if he heard a Dissenter called parson—Minister Holman knows what he's about as well as e'er a farmer in the neighbourhood.

189

He gives up five days a week to his own work, and two to the Lord's; and it is difficult to say which he works hardest at. He spends Saturday and Sunday a-writing sermons and a-visiting his flock at Hornby; and at five o'clock on Monday morning he'll be guiding his plough in the Hope Farm yonder just as well as if he could neither read nor write. . . .'

The Reverend Ebenezer Holman gave us a nod as we entered the stubble-field; and I think he would have come to meet us but that he was in the middle of giving some directions to his men. . . . That man still looked like a very powerful labourer, and had none of the precise demureness of appearance which I had always imagined was the characteristic of a minister. . . . I never saw a more powerful man—deep chest, lean flanks, well-planted head. By this time we were nearly up to him; and he interrupted himself and stepped forwards; holding out his hand to me.

'Well, this is cousin Manning, I suppose. Wait a minute, young man, and I'll put on my coat, and give you a decorous and formal welcome. But—Ned Hall, there ought to be a water-furrow across this land: it's a nasty, stiff, clayey, dauby bit of ground, and thou and I must fall to, come next Monday—I beg your pardon, cousin Manning—and there's old Jem's cottage wants a bit of thatch; you can do that job tomorrow while I am busy.' Then, suddenly changing the tone of his deep bass voice to an odd suggestion of chapels and preachers, he added, 'Now, I will give out the psalm, "Come all harmonious tongues," to be sung to "Mount Ephraim" tune.'

He lifted his spade in his hand, and began to beat time with it; the two labourers seemed to know both words and music, though I did not.

ELIZABETH GASKELL (1810—1865)

190

144.   The Reverend Bute Crawley was a tall, stately, jolly, shovel-
          hatted man. . . . At college he pulled stroke-oar in the
Christchurch boat, and had thrashed all the best bruisers of the
'town'. He carried his taste for boxing and athletic exercises into
private life: there was not a fight within twenty miles at which he was
not present, nor a race, nor a coursing match, nor a regatta, nor a ball,
nor an election, nor a visitation dinner, nor indeed a good dinner in
the whole county, but he found a means to attend it. You might see
his bay mare and gig-lamps a score of miles away from his Rectory
House, whenever there was any dinner-party at Fuddleston, or at
Roxby, or at Wapshot Hall, or at the great lords of the county, with all
of whom he was intimate. He had a fine voice; sang 'A southerly wind
and a cloudy sky'; and gave the 'whoop' in chorus with general
applause. He rode to hounds in a pepper-and-salt frock, and was
one of the best fishermen in the county. . . .

He was always in debt. It took him at least ten years to pay off his
college bills contracted during his father's life-time. In the year
179—, when he was just clear of these incumbrances, he gave the
odds of 100 to 1 (in twenties) against Kangaroo, who won the Derby.
The rector was obliged to take up the money at a ruinous interest,
and had been struggling ever since.

WILLIAM MAKEPEACE THACKERAY (1811—1863)

145.   Apart from his wife—whom he loved very dearly—Septimus
          Jones lived for two things; his work and cricket.

He was a parson, so his job in life wasn't an easy one. In fact, even
in a small country parish where homely folk dwelt, it was difficult. But
he slogged away at it; christening the babies, trying to make the
children behave themselves, marrying the serious lovers, appeasing
the quarrelsome, visiting the sick, and burying the dead.

It was wearying and often disappointing labour; but to it he
brought the courage, the optimism, the friendliness, and the

191

unselfishness of an old cricketer. And remember! Cricketers are the salt of the earth!

The Great Game—with all it used to be, still is, and ever should be—meant a tremendous lot to this plump little priest with the round red face, the bald head, the boyish smile, and the enormous hands with long fingers.

Ah, those hands! Forty years ago and more, what wizardry had they not performed with a cricket-ball. . . . Cricket was in his very being. He even preached about it, and had done for years.

'The Christian Life! What is it?' he would ask, almost fiercely from the pulpit. Then—with a beaming smile of happy conviction—he would tell them that the Christian life was courage, unselfishness, patience, love of one's fellows, a struggle against odds on a bad wicket, sometimes in poor light, against venomous bowling if the Devil was in the field, and against powerful and merciless batting if he was at the wicket. The toss was the lack of one's birth—the type of bedroom you were in. The Game was Life. The Close of Play was Death. The Reward? 'Ah, the Reward my friends!' he would say—his little eyes moist and his lips trembling. '*That* passeth all understanding!'

Yes, when Septimus Jones brought cricket into a sermon—well, it got you!

Alan Miller (1888—   )

146.   This good and gentle clergyman, whose name was Mr Mountjoy remained sufficiently boyish at the age of seventy to borrow our catapults for an occasional pot-shot at a sitting rabbit or crow. ('I deplore blood-sports,' he said, 'but you can scarcely call it a blood-sport if you never hit anything.') . . . .

One of his hobbies was keeping bees. He had about fifty hives in his garden, and told us that their total population was nearly four million. 'That's as many bees as there are people in a great city. What a vast kingdom I rule!' On the first spring days he would stand contentedly for hours watching the workers sally forth and come back with the yellow crocus-pollen upon them; but at high summer he would often load some of the hives in the back of his small open car and go prospecting far afield for patches of beanflower or clover or saintfoin, and then beg the owner's permission to leave a hive or two there so that his bees could gather the honey. It was a familiar sight to see the Rector driving down the lanes with half a dozen skeps occupying the back seat while a little swarm of his turbulent passengers rose from them like a thin smoke and swirled about his head.

He was also a keen ornithologist. I suspect that Mr Mountjoy, like another and greater parson-naturalist, took more interest in his feathered parishioners than his human ones, was less concerned with his Easter sermon than with the arrival of various little migrants about that season. Certainly he spent more time in the fields and woods than in his church or rectory. He was inordinately fond of fishing, especially pike-fishing, and it was scandalously related of him that between christenings he would keep his live bait in the font. He was often in trouble with the stricter section of his congregation for offences of this kind; his churchwardens, for instance, objected to his fixing nesting-boxes over the church porch. They declared it was unseemly. 'My dear fellows,' said Mr Mountjoy, 'can you think of anything less sacrilegious than a pair of spotted flycatchers?' Sometimes, apparently, his parishioners took their complaints to higher authority; for he confessed to us once: 'You won't see me tomorrow. I've got to go and take a wigging from the Bishop.' We feared greatly for him. 'I wonder,' said Dick, 'what the Bish will actually do to him?' But next day he was with us on the hill, unchastened and schoolboyish as ever, showing us the place where a hare ran through the hedge and telling Pistol with a wink: 'If you have any respect whatever for my cloth you will refrain from setting your wires until I am out of sight.'

JOHN MOORE (1907—1967)

147. When Jack Russell was over eighty, he started keeping a pack of harriers. The then Bishop of Exeter sent for him.
'Mr Russell, I hear you have got a pack of hounds. Is it true?'

193

'It is. I won't deny it, my lord.'

'Well, Mr Russell, it seems to me rather unsuitable for a clergyman to keep a pack. I do not ask you to give up hunting, for I know it would not be possible for you to exist without *that*. But will you, to oblige me, give up the pack?'

'Do you ask it as a personal favour, my lord?'

'Yes, Mr Russell, as a personal favour.'

'Very well, then, my lord, I will.'

'Thank you, thank you.' The Bishop, moved by his readiness, held out his hand. 'Give me your hand, Mr Russell; you are—you really are—a good fellow.'

Jack Russell gave his great fist to the Bishop, who pressed it warmly. As they thus stood, Jack said, 'I won't deceive you—not for the world, my lord. I'll give up the pack, sure enough—but Mrs Russell will keep it instead of me.'

S. BARING GOULD (1832—1924)

148.　　The Reverend Eric Wheeler was the vicar of the two parishes of Steeple and Helions Bumpstead for twenty-five years. . . . Eric was very much a man's man, not afraid to say what he thought in or out of the pulpit, who enjoyed a drink at the local, rode to hounds (Thurlow and Puckeridge), kept a horse named Bobby and a golden labrador beloved by every villager. . . . Eric Wheeler was thirteen and a wheelwright's apprentice when he became a fox-hunter, and just over twenty when he was ordained. . . .

I was sitting in my usual pew for Morning Service when in trooped a horde of unwashed strangers. They occupied the first two rows of pews just under the pulpit, and seemed to be linked together by a strange device. When Eric rose to read the lesson they rose and unfurled their banner, for that is what it was, and chanted the words printed on it; the words of Hymn No 357 . . . 'All things bright and beautiful, All creatures great and small, All things wise and wonderful, The parson kills them all.'

The intruders were of some unspecified battalion of the Hunt Saboteurs. . . . Eric was profoundly distressed and angry, for he

RIDING TO HOUNDS

loved his pair of churches. Our congregation was larger than usual and about forty of us shouted 'OUT!' Women waved umbrellas and hymn-books, men advanced with clenched fists. Violence was avoided by Ken, the village policeman. He calmed the congregation, grabbed some banner-bearers and led them from the church as other policemen arrived. Outside our church, prancing on graves, yelling and blowing horns there were others—some carrying placards: 'there's a knave in the nave', 'there's nothing sicker than a hunting vicar!', 'hunting is a clerical error'.

We returned to our pews. Eric apologized to the congregation for the interruption of our service. 'These people are only cardboard heroes and will later be ashamed for committing an act against God, His Church and us, His worshippers. I am truly grateful for your support this morning.'

SPIKE MAYS (1907—   )

149.   There is still music in Toddington, and plenty of it, too. Captious residents in the place are even heard to declare that
there is too much of it, especially on summer evenings, when the
vicar conducts his little brass band on the green. On those practice
evenings the village heart-beat quickens, as those well-known tunes
surge over the hill. There is no point in talking, then: the only thing to
do is to keep quiet, or sing with the band. Down in the valley the men
pause in their gardens. 'There's Freddie's band at it again,' they say,
trying to catch the tune as it flows down to them in waves.

'Freddie' is the vicar, and he would be the very last person to object
to such familiarity. He organised the village brass band, whose
members are drawn solely from the workers—the blacksmith, the
shepherd, old Fairy the stockman, and the lads who ride off to the
jam factory each day on noisy motor-cycles—for no other reason
than because he knows there is nothing so tonic as being able to
make a loud noise. When inviting subscriptions from the Hall, of
course, he said a band would help to hold the village together; but his
honest reason for undertaking the adventure was that he knew it
would be a handy means of letting off steam. He is fond of letting off
steam himself. . . .

So the band was started and soon became a great success. There
was never much finesse about its performances, and neither
Freddie nor his bandsmen ever showed much desire to tackle music
that wasn't chiefly noticeable for its good, broad tunes: the broader
the better. In matters of expression, maybe, it ran to extremes: its
'louds' were loud enough to blow the walls out, when it practised in
the schoolroom, and its 'softs' were a whisper to melt the heart, and
the alternations between the two extremes were swift and dramatic.

C. HENRY WARREN

150.   'My husband has asked you to stay the night, Lord Peter,' said
Mrs Venables, 'but he ought to have mentioned that you will
probably get very little sleep, being so close to the church. But
perhaps you do not mind the sound of bells.'

197

'Not at all,' said Lord Peter Wimsey.

'My husband is a very keen change-ringer,' pursued Mrs Venables, 'and, as this is New Year's Eve—'

The Rector, who seldom allowed anybody else to finish a sentence, broke in eagerly.

'We hope to accomplish a real feat to-night,' he said, 'or rather, I should say, to-morrow morning. We intend to ring the New Year in with—you are not, perhaps, aware that we possess here one of the finest rings in the country?'

'Indeed?' said Wimsey. 'Yes, I believe I have heard of the Fenchurch bells.'

'There are, perhaps, a few heavier rings,' said the Rector, 'but I hardly know where you would rival us for fullness and sweetness of tone. Number seven, in particular, is a most noble old bell, and so is the tenor. . . .'

'And have you a good set of ringers?' inquired Wimsey, politely.

'Very good indeed. Excellent fellows and most enthusiastic. That reminds me, I was about to say that we have arranged to ring the New Year in to-night with no less,' said the Rector, emphatically, 'no less than fifteen thousand, eight hundred and forty Kent Treble Bob Majors. What do you think of that? Not bad, eh?'

'Bless my heart!' said Wimsey. 'Fifteen thousand—'

'Eight hundred and forty,' said the Rector.

Wimsey made a rapid calculation.

'A good many hours' work there,'

'Nine hours,' said the Rector, with relish.

'Well done, sir,' said Wimsey. 'Why, that's equal to the great performance of the College Youths in eighteen hundred and something.'

'In 1868,' agreed the Rector. 'That is what we aim to emulate. And, whats more, but for the little help I can give, we shall be obliged to do as well as they did, and ring the whole peal with eight ringers only. We had hoped to have twelve, but unhappily, four of our best men have been laid low by this terrible influenza. . . .'

The rest of the Rector's observations on. . . change-ringing were unhappily lost, for at that moment Emily made her appearance at the door, with the ominous words:

'If you please, sir, could James Thoday speak with you for a moment?'

'*James* Thoday?' said the Rector. 'Why, certainly, of course. Put him in the study, Emily, and I will come in a moment.'

The Rector was not long gone, and when he returned his face was as long as a fiddle. He let himself drop into his chair in an attitude of utter discouragement.

'This,' he ejaculated, dramatically, 'is an irreparable disaster!'

'Good gracious, Theodore! What in the world is the matter?'

'William Thoday! Of all nights in the year! Poor fellow, I ought not to think of myself, but it is a bitter disappointment—a bitter disappointment.'

'Why, what has happened to Thoday?'

'Struck down,' said the Rector, 'struck down by this wretched scourge of influenza. Quite helpless. Delirious. . . . And there is no one now to take his place. Our grand scheme will have to be abandoned. . . . Ah, well! Man proposes and God disposes—unless'—the Rector turned suddenly and looked at his guest—'you were speaking just now with a good deal of feeling about Treble Bobs—you are not yourself, by any chance, a ringer?'

'Well,' said Wimsey, 'I used at one time to pull quite a pretty rope. But whether, at this time of day —'

'Treble Bob?' inquired the Rector, eagerly.

'Treble Bob, certainly. But it's some time since—'

'It will come back to you,' cried the Rector, feverishly. 'It will come back. Half an hour with the handbells—'

'My dear!' said Mrs Venables . . . 'is it quite fair to ask Lord Peter Wimsey, after a motor accident, and at the end of a tiring day, to stay up ringing bells from midnight to nine o'clock?'

DOROTHY L. SAYERS (1893—1957)

199

POINTERS TO THE FUTURE

6. LOOKING TO THE FUTURE

Change

151.   Until recently we were probably the only diocese in England with a Mountie vicar. Accoutred in clerical collar and jodhpurs, he did his parish rounds on a fine chestnut stallion. And what better way of visiting his flock in their sporadic hamlets, divided by our miniature mountains where the worn soil seems stretched so tight that elbows of rock stick out through the frayed rags of turf, and linked often by only spindly lanes which scrape both sides of a car. I can see that it must be less trouble than a horse, and certainly has more horsepower, but I do personally regret that the vicar has now gone over to a zippy MGB.

KENNETH ALLSOP (1920—1973)

152.   I lived in the vicarage through the beginnings of decay, but still it was a pleasant dwelling, properly related to church, village and parish all around. Through the chestnuts and gigantic laurels came the noises of a community, the sawyers in their pit on one side of the Green, the ringing of iron on iron from the two smithies, the passing of carts and waggons. The external noises were countered inside the garden by the noise of children. Within the fence, the chestnuts, the laurels, the garden remained a pleasance for meditation and seemly living, even if the weeds grew thicker on the gravel paths, the trees grew older and nearer their death, and the grass and nettles thickened around the rose-scented peonies. . . .

The second war finished off a vicarage too grandiose and a garden, or set of gardens, too big altogether for the vicar's stipend. The revolution came to a head after my father retired, and when he lay quiet at last in his own churchyard under a slate stone. First of all, the vicarage designed for several maids and a family of children was diminished by pulling down some of the rooms. The gardens were neglected absolutely. The war came, half the vicarage was unused, none of it was properly heated or maintained. Dry rot began in the cellars which once contained so much port, so much marsala and claret; and when the war was over, the church authorities were lucky enough to find a purchaser, and the vicar has to live in that cottage on the borders of his old demesne until a new and smaller vicarage can be built. An inescapable change, no doubt, though the parishioners disliked it, much as I dislike it myself. An old balance was upset, an old pattern destroyed. Their parson was in some sense dethroned.

GEOFFREY GRIGSON (1905—1985)

153.   The vicar has long since departed,
The parish is now one of six,
Parsons come not from the country,
They're foreign to life in the sticks.

And what of the Church and the fabric?
It's very much now hand to mouth,
When they couldn't repair the Church tower,
They sold the bells in the south.

It's hard for the faith in the country,
Under attack from superior forces,
Which belittle the faith of our forbears,
And seek our historic resources.

My children and their children I pray for,
They've a life that's harder to lead,

For the faith that sustained their forbears
Wilts in a climate of greed.

EDDIE ADAMS (1919—   )

154.   By 1980 Wickwyn was one of a group of eight small parishes
served by a single priest. On Sundays he was kept busy
travelling from one sparsely attended service to another; but on
weekdays, with only just over a thousand souls in his parishes, he
found himself with little to do. When asked, he readily complained of
overwork, but in truth he was so uncertain of his role and purpose
that even quite simple tasks seemed burdensome. He was relieved
that many people still sought his services for weddings and funerals,
but was inwardly hurt that at most times he was treated with benevo-
lent disregard.

ROBERT VAN DE WEYER (1950—   )

Reconstruction

155.   I am lord of all I survey. The forty square miles of beautiful
        Cotswold countryside are rich in history, church buildings,
sheep, trees and money—rich in everything except people.
Scattered around this wedge of Gloucestershire south-west of
Cirencester are about 900 people in seven separate settlements.
The largest is Coates, with a population of 300. . . . Then there is the
parish of Rodmarton—which also includes the hamlets of
Culkerton, Hazleton and Tarlton. Rodmarton (population 100) is
an estate village, where until very recently the only privately owned
house was the old rectory. . . . Sapperton and Frampton Mansell
(population 175 each) were united in 1600 and have been at enmity
ever since. One was Royalist, the other Roundhead, and so it has
gone on. . . .

Ten years ago there was a resident rector in each of the three
ecclesiastical parishes. One died, one moved, and the Rector of
Coates was forced to take on the lot. As one local put it: 'We didn't
want him and he didn't want us.' Today it is perhaps difficult to
realise what an appalling thing had happened. Two rectories had
been sold with no financial compensation to the parishes. Moreover
the resident rectors had been the lynchpins of community life for
150 years. They had built the schools and the village halls; they had
acted as social welfare officers and youth leaders; and they usually
automatically chaired the parish council as well as the PCC.
Suddenly this full-time honorary village jack-of-all-trades was gone.
It seemed inconceivable that the villages—let alone the village
churches—could survive such a blow. The fact that in our case they
did so is in great part due to the work of my predecessor. . . . In two
stormy years he established a workable pattern of services,
abolished Matins in favour of Parish Communion, and converted
from the Book of Common Prayer to Rite B. He visited virtually
everyone leaving me an excellent card index, and he spread the
word around that *things had now changed!* But no one can live with
that sort of hatchet job for long, and after two years he moved to

another benefice, leaving the parishes to lick their wounds and choose a new rector.

My wife and I came down one July day in 1978 to be interviewed by the churchwardens and PCCs. It was a terrifying experience. We were passed from one set of Cotswold grandees to another, ending up with a very sticky cross-examination by the Earl and the Admiral at Sapperton. But fortunately my wife, who is more or less a local girl, discovered a number of mutual acquaintances in the parishes, and also realised that she had once taught the children of one of the churchwardens.

As a result of all this they decided that we would do, and that since they had got a rector they could agree on, they had better bury their differences and try to make him and his family happy.

ANDREW BOWDEN (1938—   )

156.   In 1963 rumours were being circulated to the effect that the Bishop of Norwich proposed to group rural parishes—to appoint small teams of clergy, and make the laity more aware of accepting responsibility. Without grouping it is possible (in the light of previous experience) that the eight parishes would have been placed under the care of a minimum number of priests anticipating retirement, in the peace and quiet of a rural backwater.

Some of us, who were frustrated by this prospect of filling vacancies, warmed to the Bishop's idea. Because we were Norfolk people we wanted to proceed with caution. It became abundantly clear that the Group idea, like a firework once lit, was difficult to extinguish. Some of us met the Archdeacon after a festival service in September 1963 in Norwich Cathedral. He left no doubt in our minds that the idea was already in the planning stage. He named the parishes and said we would be known as 'The Hempnall Group'.

Having heard this and gone away to mull it over, we realised the many problems involved. For example, some parishes were in different deaneries. How could three parsons possibly do what, in the old days, eight priests had done? We knew nothing about lay ministry, or the keen young priests, or the mobility of dashing from

205

village to village on Honda 50 motor bikes, clad in cassock and helmet, a cardboard box on the back full of hymnbooks and a surplice or alb stuffed on top.

Shortly after our first positive meeting with the Archdeacon, a meeting was called in Hempnall Village Hall. In that dimly lit building on a typical autumn afternoon, Bishops, Churchwardens, PCCs and parishioners all met together on our first joint, memorable and historic occasion. Several points of view were aired; one of the smaller parishes voiced quite forcibly that the largest parish, Hempnall, had already given the name in the title of the Group—however, that did not imply Hempnall would dominate the situation. I remember feeling my hackles rise at this because I was churchwarden in Hempnall, and the last thing I, or my colleagues, wanted to happen was for Hempnall to have it all its own way. The Bishop explained that three men were to comprise this team; one was actually already waiting to reside among us in any of the villages where accommodation could be found. The leader planned to live in Morningthorpe and not in Hempnall. The patron for Hempnall told me afterwards that this was, in his view, the most unsatisfactory aspect of the change.

ROY LADBROOKE (1922—   )

157.   Each village, however small, is of course a unit of pastoral care and this must be taken into account in a strategy for ministry. But if the shortage of clergy today makes it necessary to link most villages up in a wider network of ministry this can be turned to advantage in helping to break down the myth of the self-contained community. Few tears should be shed over the disappearance of the late Victorian country parson, ministering for perhaps forty years or more in possession of the freehold of a single benefice. His ghost could not be comfortable in a modern-sized vicarage surrounded by executive homes and mechanised farming. . . .

But from the standpoint of the parishioners there is a change not simply in the amount but in the nature of the pastoral care being offered as soon as there is no longer a resident incumbent. To quote

Trevor Dorey, 'There is a need for an alternative door to knock on in times of crisis and for alternative eyes and ears in each place. Real community, after all, can only be fostered by local residents.'

But this is continually happening quite naturally. There is no need in a country parish to organise a sophisticated visiting scheme and an elaborate structure of street wardens. Village neighbours are inevitably aware of each other's needs. It is a question therefore of identifying those 'natural pastors' who are able to share the incumbent's aims and work with him rather than seeing him as one on whom to make demands. One particular home may become the priest's base when he is in the parish and the 'focal point' of pastoral care when he is not. Once training in shared ministry has developed the gifts of the laity contacts made through this 'focal point' need not invariably be referred to the incumbent.

It is unlikely that many smaller villages will have sufficient resources for the local Church to undertake a fully shared ministry without the support of clergy and readers drawn from elsewhere. This is not to deny the vocation of every baptised Church member. A handful of committed Christians may well feel that they lack some of the more particular gifts of leadership, teaching and pastoral care.... So a future strategy, while providing for 'focal points' in each village, must cease to think in terms of individual parish units for deployment of ministerial resources....

The conclusion we would wish to draw here is that each rural parish, as a distinct community, must remain a basic unit of pastoral care, but that ministerial resources, development and planning should be grouped to cover wider areas in which the local Church operates a shared ministry, and the deanery offers possibilities of development for this purpose.

JOHN TILLER (1938—   )

Local Ministry

158. 'What is the province of the laity? To hunt, to shoot, to enter-
      tain. These matters they understand, but to meddle with
ecclesiastical matters, they have no right at all.'

Though few . . . in any period would have agreed with this opinion of Monseigneur George Talbot, expressed in a letter to Archbishop Manning on 25 April 1857, nonetheless historically the Church of England has been a clerical church. The local village church has always been seen as 'the vicar's church' and most people subscribe to the inherited belief that religion and all matters associated with it are exclusively the parson's business . . . .

The presence of a highly trained and competent man whose role is to promote the goals of the organisation encourages those around him to leave matters entirely in his hands. . . . In former generations the professional clergyman, particularly in rural areas, with time to devote to the smallest details of church and parish life, created attitudes that have persisted. . . .

Today, leadership is much more diffuse, much less specific. In contemporary society 'the leader' is the man who has the skill, the knowledge, the ability and the personality to make the group function to the best advantage. Such 'focal persons' possess particular abilities in motivating and enabling groups to achieve their goals. They have skills to resolve the conflicts in the group, to optimize the contributions of group members, to identify the appropriate means and to marshal the required resources and knowledge. By its very nature this style of leadership is low profile and self-effacing; it is the leadership of service, and often involves shouldering the burden of responsibility for the activities and work of the group which no one else will accept. . . .

At the centre of each Christian community there is a need to develop a Ministerial Team of people who are able corporately to witness and to minister in the place where they are. It is in the context of such teams that what is often called the 'ministry of the laity' but is in truth the ministry of the whole church, will develop and grow. By God's grace the ordained priest can enable by his skills, his knowledge and his abilities the priesthood of the whole church to be manifested and exercised according to the needs of the local situation. He 'epitomises' the corporate priesthood of the church; he is the enabler of the community ministry; he is the 'animateur' of the people of God. He articulates by his holiness, humility and good sense the priesthood of the Body of Christ, and in this way he activates the People of God to fulfil their calling and vocation of ministry in the world.

ANTHONY RUSSELL (1943—   )

159.   One dejected Clergyman at least has found that watching the local cricket team helps. Coming out of the gaunt grey parish church, built to hold 300 people, and where he had one sunny summer Sunday afternoon been conducting the usual evening service for five elderly people, he stopped on his way home to watch the village cricket match, as truly part of the traditional English scene as the building he had just left. There were the eleven players, all dressed in their ritual white clothes; two umpires, local farm workers but deemed by their mates to be capable of standing up without fear or favour and making quick decisive judgements; a whole army of women who were proudly standing by the table laden with teas; and scattered around the field, a scorer with his book, a boy to put up the numbers, and some twenty or thirty spectators all of whom he knew. Apart from the visiting team and their friends, the whole group of some 50 or 60 people, were drawn from his small local village. They were all using their various talents, quite voluntarily, to arrange this ritual game at no charge to anyone, apart from what they themselves were going to pay for their teas and subscriptions; and not only had they done it in this village, but in the next, and the next, and all were knit together in a common organisation of friendly competition without any paid assistance or supervision whatsoever. It was a sobering reflection, and not one calculated to cheer him much at a time when everyone seemed to be discussing where his salary was to come from and he distinctly remembered entering the collection in his book as a few shillings.

209

There is no reason whatsoever why a non-stipendiary Presbyterate well trained and led, conscious of being part of a working team, and supported by the Laity willing to take on more and more pastoral responsibility, should not be just as efficient, if not more so, than the full time Ministers who have to spend so much of their time in irrelevant fund raising or social activities.

CHRISTOPHER DONALDSON (1918—   )

160.   As a reader in training, and thereby one who hopes to be part of the Church's proposed long-term programme for lay-dominated local ministry, I must voice my disquiet over what I perceive as an almost universal state of euphoria amongst our Church leaders in this matter. I find it totally unrealistic to anticipate that, through committed lay involvement backed by a dwindling and overstretched priestly force, the Church can expect to meet the demands which will be made on it in the coming years, leave alone grow.

Until recent retirement I spent more than thirty years in the academic study of the effectiveness of organisations and the responses to the quality and pattern of their leadership. I have never yet found an organisation with a high level of effectiveness and capacity for sustained growth except where it is managed by highly expert leaders at all levels who are committed totally to the success of that organisation and able to give it their full time and attention.

To expect that the Church can survive and even grow on the basis of a local leadership of part-timers is to live in cloud-cuckoo-land.

I believe in lay participation, but only where it is *closely* allied with highly expert and full-time professional leadership. The argument that the early church grew from amateur beginnings has simply no relevance today in the well-informed, highly sophisticated and competitive society in which we live. Congregations will only tolerate a certain level of non-availability and mediocrity from their leadership and new blood is certainly not attracted to a congregation by it.

DAVID LLOYD (1928—   )

161.   Each local church ought therefore to have within itself as part
       of itself the ministries which it needs to build itself up and
sustain its life in Christ. Whatever criticisms can be made of the
shape of the rural church in the last century, it did very largely meet
this criterion: each village gathered round its own church with its
own parson who was pastor, minister of word and sacrament, leader
and exemplar. With the removal of the one man in whom all the
functions of ministry were concentrated, many flocks are now
without shepherds, and many bodies without vital limbs and
organs. . . .

We daily accept that most of our country churches are and will
indefinitely be without priests or authorized leaders of their own,
and depend for many of their vital functions on a more or less
occasional visitor. Ministries, which should be the property of the
local church, we have packed up in a suitcase and handed over to a
travelling salesman.

The schemes that are springing up to develop lay leadership and
local non-stipendiary ministry, are moves to unpack the suitcase
and restore to the local church its rights and responsibilities. There
are two reasons why it is something of a struggle to do so, and why
the Church is so timid about it. The first is the false
professionalization to which the ministry has succumbed. Since the
nineteenth century the clergy have modelled themselves on the
secular professions, like medicine and law: clergymen have created
a mystique about their functions and status which depends on a
mysteriously acquired expertise for which they are paid, and a sense
of apartness from other men symbolized in clerical dress. None of
this really has anything to do with Christian ministry, but there are
strong resistances, especially within the profession itself, to any
deprofessionalization of its functions.

The other obstacle to the restoration of the ministry to the local
church is that many local churches in rural areas now appear unable
to produce the leaders and ministers of their own which they need.
In the pre-Nicene Church, following the pattern of the synagogue, a
Christian community of twelve heads of families could be
recognized as a church. Such a church then acquired a right to a

priest or leader, chosen from its own number, and to the celebration of the Eucharist at which he presided. But there are plenty of country churches today which would be unable to muster twelve heads of families even at Christmas or Easter. Our problem, in an age in which the Church is contracting rather than expanding, is what to do with the remnants of what were once churches, but are not viable units any longer.

MARTIN DOWN (1940—   )

162.   I went one day into a synod office in Canada. I found there two men: the one was a young theological student, the other a man of about fifty years of age who told me that for fifteen years, when he was farming on the prairie, he held services in his own house for his neighbours. At first some six or seven Anglicans came, but later some of the other people came also. They had a celebration of the Holy Communion two or three times a year when a priest passed that way.

I looked at those two men and I could not help asking myself why the bishop was going to ordain the one and why he had not ordained the other. If spiritual experience is desirable for a priest, which of those two men had the largest spiritual experience? If intellectual ability was considered, I had no doubt which of the two was the abler man: if education, a very short conversation revealed which of them was the better educated. If it is important that a parish priest should be able to lead and direct his congregation, who could question for a moment which of those two men most commanded respect? Which of them had the best and strongest social influence? The one was a married man, and his wife and children were respected in the society in which they lived: the other was unmarried and no one could foretell whom he would marry or whether his wife would be a help or a hindrance to him in his work. The diocese was understaffed, and appealing incessantly for aid in money and in men: which of these men would be the greatest burden on its scanty funds? The one was being supported as a student, and must be supported by the diocese as long as he lived, unless he went away or committed some flagrant offence: the other never had, and never would, cost the diocese a halfpenny. The one lived up-country for fifteen years, and during all that time lacked nothing but Orders to be the pastor of his flock: he would undoubtedly have built up the Church where he lived. Of the other all that could be said was that he was apparently a very respectable young man; whether he would be a leader of men, or a good parish priest, when he was forty years of age; whether he would stay more than a year or two doing up-country work; whether he would not soon be seeking a town parish, or desiring one, which would equally distract his mind from the work up-country, even it if did not result in his leaving it, who could foretell? Every one hoped for the best, but no one could be certain. All these possibilities made his training and ordination (from the point of view of a diocese which needed above all things the Church built up in small scattered groups) a pure gamble with the funds at the disposal of the diocese. No one could be sure how he would turn out. About the elder man there was not a shadow of doubt; he was no novice, he had approved himself.

Why then did the bishop not ordain that man when he was on his farm doing exactly the work which the Church needed? Why did he leave him unequipped and hampered by lack of ordination? And why was he determined to ordain only the younger man?

ROLAND ALLEN (1869—1947)

Non-stipendiary ministry

163.   If the churches are to maintain a trained ministry in the countryside, it will need to be largely unpaid. . . . Of course some
would immediately question. . . the need for a trained ministry.
They argue that house-churches, worshipping communities, base-
communities, or whatever, can function very well without a trained
ministry. They sometimes point to earliest Christianity as a
precedent for this and see clericalization as a regressive phase of
church 'development'. I accept a part of this argument. Yet I am also
aware of the social dangers that have faced religious organizations
attempting to manage without a trained ministry. . . . Sociologically,
trained leadership is important, for the identity, control,
maintenance and directionality of most social institutions. And
those British churches which have attempted to sustain their rural
congregations through a predominantly lay leadership—the
obvious example is Methodists—do not provide encouragement for
this more radical position. . . .

But from where are the churches to find a predominantly unpaid
trained ministry? Clergy frequently ask me this question, even when
they realize that I have had non-stipendiary charges in the
Edinburgh and Newcastle dioceses for the last fifteen years. On
more than one occasion my local deanery synod solemnly
discussed non-stipendiary ministry, expressing grave doubts about
whether anyone in full employment would have sufficient time for
rural ministry, even while I was sitting there. Let me suggest five
obvious sources for this form of minstry.

First, there are the stipendiary extra-parochial clergy to be found
in most churches, but present in every diocese in the Church of
England. It has always been essential to me as a priest to function as a
priest in a specific worshipping congregation. I have always been
puzzled by colleagues who are content to return to the pew or to play
a very subsidiary role from one Sunday to the next. Conducting
regular worship, preaching, celebrating the sacrament, and being
the pastor to others in and beyond the congregation, were amongst
the main reasons for offering myself for ordination. . . . Yet most

dioceses assume that some of their most senior clergy should function otherwise. . . .

Secondly, there are previously trained clergy in many churches who are employed outside the churches. For one reason or another, we trained and often functioned for a while as stipendiary clergy, but then chose to take outside employment. . . . My own 'outside employment' would traditionally not have been considered to be 'outside' at all, and I never actually left parochial ministry, only stipendiary ministry. Yet I have discovered the joys of being a country priest whilst simultaneously enjoying my university career. I believe that others could be encouraged to do this. . . . Of course such clergy need to be efficient. If their time is limited it needs to be used effectively and the ministry of the rest of the congregation needs to be mobilized. . . .

Thirdly, there are those trained especially for non-stipendiary ministry. . . . Of course. . .many. . .will need to remain in urban areas because of their paid employment. Not all of those in secular employment will be able or even willing to commute on a daily basis. Nevertheless, having done exactly that for twelve years, I know that it does work. In theory it sounds ludicrous to teach full-time in Edinburgh, yet commute daily from a rural parish in the Scottish Borders. Yet in practice it does work. . . . Clergy commuting to secular employment or to a central diocesan job, may actually identify more closely with the present-day life-styles of their parishioners than do their stipendiary rural colleagues. . . .

Fourth, there are the retired or semi-retired clergy. The Scottish Episcopal Church has made extensive use of this group of clergy to staff some of its smaller rural churches. . . . It may be difficult permanently to manage a particular church on this basis. . . . Yet for a while, and when mixed with other patterns of ministry, or even when supported by a neighbouring parish, it can be an important way of ensuring that rural congregations do have their own trained ministry. . . .

Fifthly, there might even be a group of partly-paid clergy. . . . Of course, this remuneration must come from within the rural parish itself. . . . Perhaps the more enterprising really could explore the possibility of combining a partly-paid rural ministry with other forms of remuneration. . . . A few churches are already open to this form of ministry. However, as women come to exercise a more central role in ministry, so all churches will need to become considerably more open in this respect. Currently, amongst women doctors, there is extensive discussion of the need of married women to balance their professional duties with motherhood. Many. . . general practices are discovering the gifts that a woman doctor, even working less than full-time, can bring. Churches could make a similar discovery.

ROBIN GILL (1944—   )

164.   A major aspect of the Church's response to the present crisis in stipendiary manpower has been the discovery of 'local ministry'. Local ministry involves both the recognition of the true identity and potential of the laity within the local church and the selection and training of local people for a self supporting ordained ministry. The theory and theology of local ministry are impressive. There are, however, three severe practical problems.

First, many rural churches are already too weak to produce their own leadership. These communities need the stimulus of external mission over a long period of time before the vision of local ministry can work.

Second, the village church needs to be able to compete with the high professional standards which people assume today from secular education and the media. Unless liturgy and catechesis can reach these standards, the local church will not be taken seriously.

. Third, local people carry with them inhibitory as well as enabling potential within their own community. As Jesus found in Nazareth, there is one place in which prophets find it particularly difficult to minister. The rural Free Churches relied heavily on this particular route, and many are now closed.

Local ministry and full-time stipendiary ministry will remain vital components of the rural church's future. My own vision, however, believes that it is necessary to supplement these two forms of

216

ministry with a fully professional non-stipendiary ministry which is flexible and mobile enough to be sent to live in rural communities where such a ministry is needed. It is precisely in those areas where a local ministry is lacking that ministry by a peripatetic outsider is most likely to prove ineffective.

I have fulfilled my own ministry as a non-stipendiary priest in this way. It is hard work, but rewarding. It is a ministry which is only made possible by the support of local lay ministers and the assistance of neighbouring stipendiary ministers.

At the end of the Victorian era, the rural church was rich in terms of plant, through the restoration and enrichment of the village churches and the consolidation of the rural parsonages.

The fine churches still remain. A combination of local, diocesan and national resources are directed to their upkeep. . . . At the same time, with a thirty per cent. reduction in the stipendiary clergy, a rural diocese has also lost thirty per cent. of its parsonage houses within a relatively short period of time.

While the churches are preserved . . . on a typical Sunday eighteen per cent. will not be used at all and a further fifty-seven per cent. will be used for only one service. Twenty-four per cent. of the services will attract congregations of ten or less. Clearly the surviving plant is not proving that useful. It is true that gothic churches are powerful symbols of the Christian presence; but I suspect that symbolism and nostalgia will not carry the church all that far into the twenty-first century.

What the rural church needs today is a warm, welcoming and comfortable environment in which children can explore the faith and in which adults can meet, learn and worship. Strangely, the parsonage can provide such an environment.

The theory of local ministry suggests that local homes can provide as good an environment as the parsonage. Unfortunately, local relationships often get in the way of such a theory working in practice, even when a home of an appropriate size is available. The parsonage, like the church itself, can be seen as neutral territory, public property. It is difficult for a private home to be seen in this way, except among the most committed.

I have fulfilled my own non-stipendiary ministry from the local parsonage house, which had not yet been disposed of after the withdrawal of the last stipendiary incumbent. The form of ministry I have been able to offer has been quite different from that of the full-time clergy who occupied the house before me, but the parsonage itself has continued to be a valuable resource for the local church and for the wider community.

I am left wondering, therefore, whether the rural church might have been wiser to spend its limited resources not on maintaining medieval churches, but on adapting the parsonage house for the needs of the living Christian community and training a new generation of non-stipendiary clergy to resource these homes as centres for Christian nurture and witness.

LESLIE J. FRANCIS (1947—   )

165.   John and Veronica Strong with their three children live in the village of Harlington, where John is priest-in-charge, and he works in a Luton factory checking oil meters, travelling to and from work each day with most of his male parishioners. He does a full Sunday's work in the parish church and keeps up with his sick visiting and other routine duties of a parish priest . . . .

Naturally we are asked many questions about our work. . . . 'What do your workmates think of you?' is perhaps the favourite. They accept us first and foremost as ordinary human beings—one of themselves. . . . But quite a few have said, 'Well, if anyone could persuade me to believe in religion it would be someone like you.'

DAVID L. EDWARDS (1929—   )

166.   Establishment has meaning not only at a national level, but also locally. This local understanding of the relationship between the Church of England and the community as a whole is symbolised in the unconscious but significant difference in the way the average Church of England clergyman talks of his responsibilities, compared with the clergy of other denominations. . . . The Church of England clergyman has an instinctive perception that his responsibilties extend throughout a geographical area, irrespective of the religious commitment of his parishioners. . . .

It still remains true that the bishop is regarded as a leadership figure in the county in which his diocese is set. He will be invited to a variety of events in the area, and to identify himself with a wide range of causes which have no necessary connection with his ecclesiastical functions. He is invited by virtue of his 'establishment' status. For most bishops this kind of involvement beyond the boundaries of the church forms an important part of his ministry, for it provides an understanding of the community as a whole—an understanding which is vital for his effective leadership of the church—and also affords the possibility of influencing in certain ways the course of affairs in a region.

Parallel opportunities exist for the Church of England parish priest, especially in rural areas. By virtue of his title of 'Vicar' or 'Rector' he has an almost unlimited entrée into the homes of his parish and, if he wishes, to the clubs, societies and institutions that are the focal points for the corporate life of the local community. It is to him that people come at special times in their lives: for baptisms, marriages and funerals. In return for this admission to the community as a whole, he is expected to care for the whole community. This right of entry and the priest's response to it has changed in recent years to some extent. The process of secularisation has had the effect, especially in urban areas, that the local vicar is not regarded so much as the man who belongs to all the people: those of other faiths and of no faith do not necessarily welcome the Church of England clergyman nor expect him to minister in any way to them. Nevertheless the tradition has remarkable persistence in many rural areas where the expectations are little changed from those of a century ago. More often nowadays it is not so much the expectations of parishioners that have changed as the clergyman's understanding of his role. . . .

The 'quiet country living' simply does not exist any more. The numbers of people and the geographical area of a country clergyman's responsibility has been dramatically increased in a comparatively short period. Obviously the traditional expectations of rural parishioners cannot be fulfilled by their clergy in these new circumstances. In particular, the community role of the country parson is changing, for he no longer has the time, with his much greater responsibilities, to identify with the range of village activities that has been the historic role of his predecessors for generations.

PETER NOTT (1933—)

167.   For generations, people have tended to look upon the life of the country clergyman as quiet and uneventful, slow-paced and undemanding. . . . Today churchwardens realistically appreciate that it needs a fit and energetic man to carry out the duties of a modern country clergyman. While, generations ago in Warwickshire, when people wished to denote scarcity, they remarked 'as rare as sweat on a parson's brow'; today it is more common to find a clergyman rushing from one engagement to another in a week of constant activity and to hear him remark ruefully that a course in rally driving would be an appropriate addition to the theological college curriculum. Far from being the Church's least demanding and most generalized ministry, ministry in the countryside has becomes increasingly specialised. . . .

Today the country clergyman's role is to foster, encourage and develop the life of the local church in the villages he serves, which must necessarily grow to the point where they are no longer immediately dependent for every aspect of their life on his energy and initiative. Leadership must be shared by the clergyman with members of the congregation who, together, form a ministerial team jointly responsible for the life and witness of the church in the area. . . .

It is possible to identify four principal roles which the modern rural clergyman must perform. First, it is his responsibility to call the local ministry of the church into being, to train and to-foster it. . . . Inevitably conflicts will arise within any group of people (and small churches at times can be smallminded) and the priest has an important role in containing and minimizing their disruptive effects, in order that the team may function to the best possible advantage. . . . Second, it is the stipendiary clergyman's role to help the local church to define and set its goals; rather, to ensure that the church continues to fulfil its ancient functions as a church. Local churches, like other organisations, frequently need someone to tell them that what they most desire may not be in their best interests and that they are departing from their original goals. . . . Third, it is the stipendiary priest's task to provide the insights and knowledge which the team needs. . . . The stipendiary clergyman has had the theological education and has the time to continue his studies, and he must act as the resource for the local church. . . . Fourth, it is the stipendiary clergyman's role to take ultimate responsibility for the work of the Church in that area. . . . Today, this role is of increasing rather than diminishing importance, for as the Church at the local level becomes increasingly similar to a voluntary associational organisation, it could become as fragile and transient as are many such organisations. It is the presence of a person charged with the ultimate care and responsiblity for the Church in a particular area which prevents this happening.

ANTHONY RUSSELL (1943—   )

168.   I personally expect with some confidence that women will be admitted to the Order of Priests during the period covered by this report. . . . This is the one way in which the numbers of stipendiary clergy could be rapidly increased: there are existing women ministers . . . who in most cases have been fully trained to the

requirements for ordinands, and in many cases are conscious of a call to ordination as priests. The number of women candidates has greatly increased in recent years, and there is good hope that future combined numbers of men and woman offering for stipendiary ministry would be well up to the target range of 400/450 recommendations each year. Moreover, the cost to the Church of training and maintaining such numbers in the stipendiary ministry would be little affected, because the stipendiary women ministers *already exist*: it is simply a question of whether they are to be priests or not.

JOHN TILLER (1938—   )

169. In recent years there has been a much wider recognition of the scandal of denominationalism and the fact that the maintenance of different denominational churches in small villages is not just practically impossible but also theologically wrong, whatever the context. At the same time the barriers that once divided denominations have been gradually perceived to be of less significance than was at one time thought, and thus a new atmosphere of ecumenical co-operation has grown up in many areas.

At the same time the increasing cost of maintaining both the ministry and the many church buildings in rural areas has disposed the churches towards rationalization. It is not uncommon for a Anglican clergyman criss-crossing his group of eight to ten country parishes to lead worship in five or six churches on a Sunday, to wave to his Methodist colleague on more than one occasion as he fulfils a similar programme over an even wider area. The recognition of such a situation argues for a rationalization of ministry. At the same time the cost of maintaining buildings and the burden this places on small congregations has also accelerated the process of ecumenical co-operation in many rural areas. Increasingly small congregations in the same village co-operate by using the larger parish church during the summer months and the smaller, more easily heated chapel during the winter months.

ANTHONY RUSSELL (1943—   )

222

170. Unpaid, part-time clergy—non-stipendiary ministers, in
      England—have become familiar figures in many parishes in
the past couple of decades. During the day they do the secular work
that earns them a living: a lot of them are teachers, though the total
spread of trades represented is wide. At evenings and weekends
they are available as clergy; and some of them for longer than that,
being already pensioned. The reasons for the new pattern are clear
enough. Over the centuries the clergy have moved from being the
only educated people in society to being one educated group
among many. Even theologically, laypeople are better educated
than they were. They also live longer than they did, and yet
sometimes retire earlier, so that in the latter third or so of their active
lives they can represent an under-used supply of intellectual energy.

At the same time, the stock of paid, full-time priests has suffered a
falling off. It is sufficiently explained by falling numbers of steady
worshippers, who are both the source and the main economic
support of a full-time ministry. This falling off has been particularly
marked in the English countryside. The old ideal of a priest in each
parish has always been patchily upheld; but in the past generation it
has broken down altogether, and groups of as many as ten villages
have been gathered into the care of ministers working as a team or
even by themselves. Team arrangements do at any rate relieve the
loneliness of the clerical life, and they deliver a parish from falling
into the hands of a single unchanging incompetent; but they are not
liked. Most parishioners would much rather have their own
ministers again.

So a supply encounters a demand. The use made of the supply
will undoubtedly grow. More and more part-timers will be recruited,
and more and more of them will have charge of parishes of their
own.

JOHN WHALE (1931—   )

171. A priest is called by God to work with the bishop and with his
      fellow-priests, as servant and shepherd among the people to
whom he is sent. He is to proclaim the word of the Lord, to call his

hearers to repentance, and in Christ's name to absolve, and to declare the forgiveness of sins. He is to baptize, and prepare the baptized for Confirmation. He is to preside at the celebration of the Holy Communion. He is to lead his people in prayer and worship, to intercede for them, to bless them in the name of the Lord, and to teach and encourage by word and example. He is to minister to the sick, and prepare the dying for their death. He must set the Good Shepherd always before him as the pattern of his calling, caring for the people committed to his charge, and joining with them in a common witness to the world.

In the name of our Lord we bid you remember the greatness of the trust now to be committed to your charge, about which you have been taught in your preparation for this ministry. You are to be messengers, watchmen, and stewards of the Lord; you are to teach and to admonish, to feed and to provide for the Lord's family, to search for his children in the wilderness of this world's temptations and to guide them through its confusions, so that they may be saved through Christ for ever.

THE ALTERNATIVE SERVICE BOOK (1980)

225

SOURCES

1 The Ordering of Priests, *Book of Common Prayer*, 1662
2 *Jude the Obscure*, Harmondsworth, Penguin, 1978
3 *Mansfield Park*, Harmondsworth, Penguin, 1966
4 'A tragedy of two ambitions', *The Distracted Preacher and Other Tales*, Harmondsworth, Penguin, 1971
5 'The priesthood', *The Poems of George Herbert*, Oxford, Oxford University Press, 1961
6 *Framley Parsonage*, Harmondsworth, Penguin, 1984
7 *Essex Eccentrics*, Ipswich, the Boydell Press, 1975
8 *Hedingham Harvest*, London, Arrow Books, 1978
9 *The Romance of the Ministry*, Boston, Pilgrim Press, 1944
10 *Barchester Towers*, Harmondsworth, Penguin, 1982
11 *Emmerdale Farm: the couple at Demdyke Row*, London, Star, 1979
12 *From Ploughboy to Priest*, Bideford, Charles Herridge, 1984
13 *The Diary of a Country Priest*, London, Fontana, 1956
14 *Freedom of the Parish*, London, Phoenix House, 1954
15 *The Bird in the Tree*, London, Coronet Books, 1967
16 *Akenfield*, Harmondsworth, Penguin, 1969
17 *A Priest to the Temple*, 1632
18 *Old Oak: the story of a forest village*, Northampton, Burlington Press, 1982
19 *A Sunset Touch*, London, William Collins, 1955
20 *Some East Anglian Clergy*, London, Faith Press, 1961
21 *Pride and Prejudice*, Harmondsworth, Penguin, 1972
22 *Doctor Thorne*, Oxford, Oxford University Press, 1980
23 'Mulliner's Buck-U-Uppo', *The World of Wodehouse Clergy*, London, Hutchinson, 1984
24 *The Vicar of Wakefield*, Harmondsworth, Penguin, 1982

25 *The Way of All Flesh*, Harmondsworth, Penguin, 1966
26 *The Importance of Being Earnest*, London, Methuen, 1988
27 *Cranford*, Harmondsworth, Penguin, 1976
28 *Emma*, Harmondsworth, Penguin, 1966
29 *The Curate's Wife*, London, Virago, 1985
30 *Vanity Fair*, Harmondsworth, Penguin, 1968
31 'Bed among the lentils', *Talking Heads*, London,
       BBC Books, 1988
32 *North and South*, Harmondsworth, Penguin, 1970
33 'The women of the vicarage', *Crucible*, vol. 24,
       pages 77-85, 1985
34 *North and South*, Harmondsworth, Penguin, 1970
35 *Imogen*, London, Corgi, 1979
36 *The Way of All Flesh*, Harmondsworth, Penguin, 1966
37 *Cranford*, Harmondsworth, Penguin, 1976
38 *Emma*, Harmondsworth Penguin, 1966
39 *Barchester Towers*, Harmondsworth, Penguin, 1982
40 *Portrait of a Village*, London, Heinemann, 1937
41 *House in Dormer Forest*, London, Jonathan Cape, 1937
42 *Adam Bede*, Harmondsworth, Penguin, 1980
43 *A Month in the Country*, Harmondsworth, Penguin, 1980
44 *Don't Upset the Choir*, Oxford, Mowbray, 1962
45 *The Vicar of Bullhampton*, Oxford, Oxford University
       Press, 1988
46 *A Son of the Rectory*, Gloucester, Alan Sutton, 1982
47 *Child of Gentle Courage*, London, Elek Books, 1974
48 Donald Gibson (ed), *A Parson in the Vale of the White Horse:
       George Woodward's letters from East Hendred 1753-61*,
       Gloucester, Alan Sutton, 1982
49 'The son's veto', *The Distracted Preacher and Other Tales*,
       Harmondsworth, Penguin, 1979
50 *Vet in Green Pastures*, London, Souvenir Press, 1985
51 *A Sunset Touch*, London, William Collins, 1955
52 *The Deserted Village*, Newbridge, Co. Kildare,
       Goldsmith Press, 1974
53 Dorothy Wise (ed), *Diary of William Tayler, Footman 1837*,
       London, The St Marylebone Society, 1987
54 *An Hour-Glass on the Run*, London, Robert Hale, 1959
55 *Middlemarch*, Oxford, Oxford University Press, 1947

56 John Beresford (ed), *The Diary of a Country Parson*,
        Oxford, Oxford University Press, 1935
57 *Scenes of Clerical Life*, Harmondsworth, Penguin, 1973
58 *A Clergyman's Daughter*, Harmondsworth, Penguin, 1964
59 'The parson's case', *Jonathan Swift: the complete poems*,
        Harmondsworth, Penguin, 1983
60 'The character of a good parson', *John Dryden*,
        Oxford, Oxford University Press, 1987
61 Donald Gibson (ed), *A Parson in the Vale of the White Horse:
        George Woodward's letters from East Hendred 1753-61*,
        Gloucester, Alan Sutton, 1982
62 Brigitte Mitchell and Hubert Penrose (eds), *Letters from
        Bath 1766-1767 by the Rev. John Penrose*,
        Gloucester, Alan Sutton, 1983
63 *Mansfield Park*, Harmondsworth, Penguin, 1966
64 *Scenes of Clerical Life*, Harmondsworth, Penguin, 1973
65 *Paradise Postponed*, Harmondsworth, Penguin, 1985
66 *Old Country Life*, London, Methuen, 1890
67 *Scenes of Clerical Life*, Harmondsworth, Penguin, 1973
68 *The Village: time of change*, London, Sphere, 1980
69 *A Clergyman's Daughter*, Harmondsworth, Penguin, 1964
70 *Crome Yellow*, London, Panther Books, 1977
71 Alan Sutton (ed), *Rural Rides of the Bristol Churchgoer*,
        Gloucester, Alan Sutton, 1982
72 *The History of Bagendon*, Cheltenham, Thomas Hailing, 1932
73 *Letters and Prose Writings*, Oxford,
        Oxford University Press, 1979
74 W. Plomer (ed), *Kilvert's Diary 1870-1879*,
        Harmondsworth, Penguin, 1977
75 *Don't Upset the Choir*, Oxford, Mowbray, 1962
76 Alan Sutton (ed), *Rural Rides of the Bristol Churchgoer*,
        Gloucester, Alan Sutton, 1982
77 *Microcosmography*, Cambridge,
        Cambridge University Press, 1897
78 *The Sketch Book*, Oxford, Oxford University Press, 1912
79 *A Handful of Dust*, Harmondsworth, Penguin, 1963
80 *The Mill on the Floss*, Harmondsworth, Penguin, 1979
81 'A tragedy of two ambitions', *The Distracted Preacher
        and Other Tales*, Harmondsworth, Penguin, 1979

82 'The great sermon handicap', *The World of Wodehouse Clergy*, London, Hutchinson, 1984
83 Jack Ayres (ed), *Paupers and Pig Killers: the diary of William Holland, a Somerset Rector 1799-1818*, Harmondsworth, Penguin, 1986
84 John Beresford (ed), *The Diary of a Country Parson*, Oxford, Oxford University Press, 1935
85 *Far from the Madding Crowd*, Harmondsworth, Penguin, 1978
86 *Oh! To Be in England*, London, Michael Joseph, 1963
87 *Old Country Life*, London, Methuen, 1890
88 Howard and Peter Coombs (ed), *Journal of a Somerset Rector 1803-1834*, Oxford, Oxford University Press, 1984
89 *The Ingoldsby Legends*, London, Richard Bentley, 1881
90 *Village Tales*, London, Breslich and Foss, 1984
91 Alan Sutton (ed), *Rural Rides of the Bristol Churchgoer*, Gloucester, Alan Sutton, 1982
92 'Blame the vicar', *Church Poems*, London, Pan, 1981
93 *Rural Anglicanism: a future for young Christians?* London, Collins Liturgical Publications, 1985
94 'Verses spoken extempore by Dean Swift on his curate's complaint of hard duty', *Jonathan Swift: the complete poems*, Harmondsworth, Penguin, 1983
95 *Lark Rise to Candleford*, Harmondsworth, Penguin, 1973
96 William Plomer (ed), *Kilvert's Diary 1870-1879*, London, Jonathan Cape, 1944
97 *Reuben's Corner*, Andover, Eyre and Spottiswoode, 1969
98 *Nightmare Abbey*, Harmondsworth, Penguin, 1969
99 *The Diary of a Farmer's Wife 1796-1797*, Harmondsworth, Penguin, 1981
100 *The Tenant of Wildfell Hall*, Harmondsworth, Penguin, 1979
101 'The Christmas dinner', Godfrey Smith (ed), *The Christmas Reader*, Harmondsworth, Penguin, 1986
102 Pamela Horn, *A Georgian Parson and his Village: the story of David Davies*, Sutton Courtenay, Beacon Publications, 1981
103 *Victorian Country Parsons*, London, Constable, 1977
104 Jack Ayres (ed), *Paupers and Pig Killers: the diary of William Holland, a Somerset Rector 1799-1818*, Harmondsworth, Penguin, 1986
105 *Henry Esmond*, Harmondsworth, Penguin, 1970

106   Michael Brander, *The Country Divine*,
        Edinburgh, Saint Andrew Press, 1981
107   'The vicar', *The Poems of Winthrop Mackworth Praed*,
        London, Walter Scott Publishing, 1903
108   'The village', *The Complete Poetical Works*,
        Oxford, Oxford University Press, 1988
109   *The Way of All Flesh*, Harmondsworth, Penguin, 1966
110   *From Ploughboy to Priest*, Bideford, Charles Herridge, 1984
111   Michael Brander, *The Country Divine*,
        Edinburgh, Saint Andrew Press, 1981
112   *The Land Endures*, London, Macdonald and Janes, 1978
113   'The village', *The Complete Poetical Works*,
        Oxford, Oxford University Press, 1988
114   *Wuthering Heights*, Harmondsworth, Penguin, 1965
115   *Village Tales*, London, Breslich and Foss, 1984
116   *The Spectator*, No. 115
117   *Letters and Prose Writings*,
        Oxford, Oxford University Press, 1979
118   *Silas Marner*, Harmondsworth, Penguin, 1967
119   Howard and Peter Coombs (ed), *Journal of a Somerset
        Rector 1803-1834*, Oxford, Oxford University Press, 1984
120   *Adam Bede*, Harmondsworth, Penguin, 1980
121   *The Vicar of Bullhampton*,
        Oxford, Oxford University Press, 1988
122   *Small Talk at Wreyland*,
        Cambridge, Cambridge University Press, 1926
123   *Village School*, Harmondsworth, Penguin, 1960
124   *Lark Rise to Candleford*,
        Oxford, Oxford University Press, 1939
125   *Under the Greenwood Tree*, Harmondsworth, Penguin, 1978
126   *Country Parson*, London, Herbert Jenkins, 1961
127   *A Few Green Leaves*, London, Grafton Books, 1981
128   *The Lord of the Harvest*, Ipswich, Boydell Press, 1983
129   William Plomer (ed), *Kilvert's Diary 1870-1879*,
        London, Jonathan Cape, 1944
130   *Hodge and His Masters*, London, Quartet, 1979
131   *Under the Greenwood Tree*, Harmondsworth, Penguin, 1978
132   *Afoot in England*, Oxford, Oxford University Press, 1982
133   *Hogs at the Honeypot*, Bee Books New and Old, 1981

134 *Victorian Country Parsons*, London, Constable, 1977
135 June E. Chatfield (ed), *The Illustrated Natural History
        of Selborne*, London, Papermac, 1984
136 *Joseph Andrews*, Oxford, Oxford University Press, 1966
137 *Gryll Grange*, Oxford, Oxford University Press, 1987
138 'The parish register', *The Complete Poetical Works*,
        Oxford, Oxford University Press, 1988
139 *Mansfield Park*, Harmondsworth, Penguin, 1966
140 *The Mill on the Floss*, Harmondsworth, Penguin, 1979
141 *Framley Parsonage*, London, Harmondsworth, Penguin, 1984
142 *Joseph Andrews*, Oxford, Oxford University Press, 1966
143 *Cousin Phillis*, Harmondsworth, Penguin, 1976
144 *Vanity Fair*, Harmondsworth, Penguin, 1968
145 *Close of Play*, St Hugh's Press, 1949
146 *Brensham Village*, London, Collins, 1946
147 *Old Country Life*, London, Methuen, 1890
148 *Return to Anglia*, London, Futura, 1986
149 *England is a Village*, London, Eyre & Spottiswoode, 1940
150 *The Nine Taylors*, London, Victor Gollancz, 1934
151 *In the Country*, London, Hamish Hamilton, 1972
152 *Freedom of the Parish*, London, Phoenix House, 1954
153 'A countryman's thoughts after reading John Betjeman's
        "Church Poems" ', *A Better Country*, vol. 15, page 28, 1988
154 *Wickwyn: a vision of the future*, London, SPCK, 1986
155 John Richardson (editor), *Ten Rural Churches*,
        Eastbourne, MARC, 1988
156 'A churchwarden remembers', Anthony Lathe (editor),
        The Group: the story of eight country churches,
        Hempnall, Hempnall Group Council, 1986
157 *A Strategy for the Church's Ministry*,
        London, CIO Publishing, 1983
158 'The clergyman's role in a layman's church', *Kingdom and
        Ministry*, Blandford, Tomorrow's Church Group, 1979
159 *Rising from the Root*,
        Beaminster, Beaminster Area Team Publication, 1985
160 Letter to *Church Times*, 2 August 1985
161 'The shape of the rural church',
        Theology, vol. 87, pages 164-172, 1984
162 *The Case for Voluntary Clergy*,

London, Eyre & Spottiswoode, 1930
163 *Beyond Decline: a challenge to the churches*,
      London, SCM, 1988
164 'Rural Anglicanism: research and vision',
      Church Times, 20 September 1985
165 *Priests and Workers*, London, SCM, 1961
166 'The establishment of the Church of England: its
      local meaning', *Occasional papers on the Rural Church*,
      volume 1, Aylsham, The Norfolk Churches Trust Ltd, 1988
167 *The Country Parish*, London, SPCK, 1986
168 *A Strategy for the Church's Ministry*,
      London, CIO Publishing, 1983
169 *Christian Unity in the Village*,
      London, British Council of Churches, 1987
170 *The Future of Anglicanism*, Oxford, Mowbray, 1988
171 Ordination of Priests, *The Alternative Service Book, 1980*
      Ordination of Priests

ACKNOWLEDGEMENTS

In addition to the acknowledgements and information given in the section on sources, the publisher and editor would like to acknowledge the following permission to reproduce copyright material. All possible attempts have been made to contact copyright holders and to acknowledge their copyright correctly. We are grateful to: Eddie Adams for A countryman's thoughts after reading John Betjeman's "Church Poems"; Alan Sutton for Aubrey Moore, *A Son of the Rectory*; BBC Enterprises Ltd for Alan Bennett, *Talking Heads*; Beacon Publications for Pamela Horn, *A Georgian Parson and his Village*; Bee Books New and Old for Frank Vernon, *Hogs at the Honey Pot*; The Bodley Head and the estate of Georges Bernanos for Georges Bernanos, *The Country Parson*; British Council of Churches for Anthony Russell, *Christian Unity in the Village*; Cassell for Anthony Russell, *Kingdom and Ministry*; Century Hutchinson for P G Wodehouse, *The World of Wodehouse Clergy*; Chatto and Windus and Mrs Laura Huxley for Aldous Huxley, *Crome Yellow*; Church House Publishing for John Tiller, *A Strategy for the Church's Ministry*; Church House Publishing on behalf of the Central Board of Finance of the Church of England for *Alternative Service Book 1980*; Church Times for Leslie J Francis, Rural Anglicanism: research and vision; Collins Publishers for John Moore, *Brensham Village* and Leslie J Francis, *Rural Anglicanism*; Collins Publishers and David Higham Associates Ltd for Howard Spring, *A Sunset Touch*; Constable Publishers for Brenda Colloms, *Victorian Country Parsons* and Geoffrey Robinson, *Hedingham Harvest*; Crucible for John Rogan, *The Women of the Vicarage*; Christopher Donaldson for *Rising from the Root*; Gerald

Duckworth and Co Ltd for Elizabeth Goudge, *The Bird in the Tree*; Eyre and Spottiswoode for C Henry Warren, *England is a Village* and Spike Mays, *Reuben's Corner* and Roland Allen, *The Case for Voluntary Clergy*; Hamish Hamilton Ltd for Kenneth Allsop, *In the Country*; Harvester Press Ltd for J L Carr, *A Month in the Country*; Heinemann and David Higham Associates Ltd for Francis Brett Young, *Portrait of a Village*; John Murray for John Betjeman, Blame the vicar, *Church Poems*; Kingsway for John Richardson, *Ten Rural Churches*; Ray Ladbrook for A churchwarden remembers, *The Group*; David Lloyd for letter to *Church Times*; MacDonald for Mary E Pearce, *The Land Endures*; Macmillan for Barbara Pym, *A Few Green Leaves*; Martin Secker and Warburg, A M Heath and the estate of the late Sonia Brownell Orwell for George Orwell, *A Clergyman's Daughter*; Michael Joseph Ltd for Miss Read, *Village School*; Michael Joseph Ltd and the estate of H E Bates for H E Bates, *Oh to be in England*; A R Mowbray and Co Ltd for Reginald Frary, *Don't Upset the Choir* and John Whale, *The Future of Anglicanism*; Peter Nott for *Occasional Papers on the Rural Church*, volume 1; Oxford University Press for Flora Thompson, *Lark Rise to Candleford*; Penguin Books Ltd for Mollie Preston's Anne Hughes, *The Diary of a Farmer's Wife 1796-1797*; Penguin Books and A D Peters and Co Ltd for John Mortimer, *Paradise Postponed*; Penguin Books Ltd and David Higham Associates Ltd for Ronald Blythe, *Akenfield*; F W Pennington for *From Ploughboy to Priest*; A D Peters and Co Ltd for Evelyn Waugh, *A Handful of Dust*; Robert Hale Limited for Allan Jobson, *An Hour-Glass on the Run*; SCM Press Ltd for David L Edwards, *Priests and Workers* and Robin Gill, *Beyond Decline*; The Society of the Faith for Charles Linnell, *Some East Anglian Clergy*; SPCK for Anthony Russell, *The Country Parish* and Robert Van de Weyer, *Wickwyn*; Souvenir Press Ltd for Hugh Lasgarn, *Vet in Green Pastures*; Sphere Books Ltd for Mary Fraser, *The Village: time of change*; Victor Gollancz Ltd for Spike Mays, *Return to Anglia*; Victor Gollancz Ltd and David Higham Associates Ltd for Dorothy L Sayers, *The Nine Taylors*; Virago Press for E H Young, *The Curate's Wife*; The Henry Williamson estate for Henry Williamson, *Village Tales*.

INDEX

All numbers in this index refer to the numbers given to the extracts
and not to pages.